New Wineskins

Faithful Mission in the 21st Century

Rena M. Yocom
editor

General Board of Global Ministries
The United Methodist Church
New York

New Wineskins: Faithful Mission in the 21st Century and Teacher's Guide

copyright © 1999 General Board of Global Ministries, The United Methodist Church

A publication of The General Board of Global Ministries, The United Methodist Church, 475 Riverside Drive, New York, NY 10115

Printed in the United States of America
ISBN 1-890569-13-5

Cover design: Edward A. Moultrie

All biblical quotations, unless otherwise noted, are from the New Revised Standard Version (NRSV) of the Bible, copyright© 1989 by the Division of Christian Education of the National Council of the Churches of Christ in the United States of America. Used by permission. All rights reserved.

Contents

Preface vi
Acknowledgments vii

1 Eve of a New Millennium
Introduction 1
Called into God's Mission 2
    Rena M. Yocom
The Transfiguration of Mission 5
    Wilbert R. Shenk
Missional Church: From Sending to Being Sent 6
    Darrell L. Guder
The Transformational Role of the Church in Angola 9
    Bishop Emilio J. M. De Carvalho

2 The Sent People of God
Introduction 11
Missionary 12
    Ronald E. Osborn
American Women in Mission 15
    Dana L. Robert
Crossing Borders 20
    Glory E. Dharmaraj
The Pattern of the Christian World Mission 24
    Lesslie Newbigin
Recruitment of Protestant Missionaries 26
    Joan Delaney, MM
Contextualization in Mission 28
    Donald R. Jacobs
Case Study: "Singing the Lord's Song" 31
    Thomas H. Graves and Alan Neely

3 A Shifting Global Context
Introduction 34
What Is a Context? 34
    Alan Neely
The North American Context 36
    Andrew Walls

Church: A "place where . . ." 38
   George R. Hunsberger

Emerging Trends in Context 39
   Stan Skreslet

A Changed Context 42
   Lesslie Newbigin

Islam: A Major Factor for the 21st Century 43
   Stan Skreslet

Mission and Transformation: A Southeast Asian Perspective 45
   Robert Solomon

Relating to People of Other Religions 47
   M. Thomas Thangaraj

Case Study: "What's the Matter, Abdaraman?" 51
   Alan Neely

4 Missional Challenges for the 21st Century

Globalization, Wealth, and Media

Introduction 55

Challenges in the Context of Globalization .55
   Sara Bhattacharji

Communication and Human Dignity 57
   William Fore

Globalization and Communitarianism 59
   Jan Love

Church in a Market Economy 62
   George R. Hunsberger

Populations, Affluence, and Distribution of Resources 63
   Randolph Nugent

The Church of the Future: A View from Africa 66
   Mercy Amba Oduyoye

Welcoming the Stranger

Who Comes in the Name of the Lord?. 68
   Harold J. Recinos

Amazing Grace 71
   Jonathan Kozol

Economic Refugees 74
   Stan Skreslet

Bridges in Spirituality 75
    Gladys McCue Taylor and Gladys Taylor Cook

God's World, Our Stewardship

EarthCurrents 77
    Howard Snyder

Earthkeeping 80
    M. L. Daneel

Healing and Reconciliation

No Nonpersons in God's Family 83
    Donald E. Messer

Forgiveness and Reconciliation 86
    Ngoy Daniel Mulunda-Nyanga

Tending God's Children

Children and Poverty: An Episcopal Initiative 89

The Shape of Your Mountain 91
    Mary Taylor Previte

Case Study: A Challenge to the Cuban Church 93
    Héctor Méndez

5 Our Engagement in Mission

Introduction 97

Learning by Apprenticeship 97
    Tex Sample

Mission from the Margins to the Margins 100
    Samuel Escobar

Mission Evangelization in Secular Societies 102
    Lesslie Newbigin

The Global Nature of the Church 104
    Robert Harman

Joy in Receiving 105
    Edward W. Poitras

Case Study: "A Church for All People?" 109
    Garnett E. Foster

Study Guide *113*

Notes *141*

Preface

Welcome to this study and welcome to this moment in Christian mission. For two thousand years we have struggled to be faithful Christians. For one thousand years we have wrestled with the question of the rightful relationship between faith and various political systems in Western Christendom. For five hundred years we have worked to discern what it means to be Protestant and how to join others who view Christianity from a different perspective. For two hundred years we have articulated our unique missional contributions as members of the Methodist or Wesleyan family in the larger Christian community.

During the course of these years, the context and form for mission have varied. Even Peter and Paul, both committed to spreading the word about the risen and living Christ, found that they each had a different context for their ministry. Likewise, John Wesley, Philip Otterbein, Melville Cox, and Lucy Rider Meyer each had a unique setting and expression of mission.

There are moments in our lives that beg for reflection: New Year's Eves, graduations, anniversaries, fortieth and fiftieth birthdays. The eve of the third millennium is also such an occasion. It is not simply one night out of 730,000; it is like the moment when an artist stands before a blank canvas or a conductor stands before a symphony orchestra ready to start the music with the baton. What must emerge is the art or music, the expression of the soul, the passion of the Christian for mission.

The new millennium will incorporate our past, but it will be changed. We live in a new age. We are not asked to replicate the past, but to find what is vital and relevant in the context of the twenty-first century, just as Christians did in the first century.

This study book presents a unique approach. The format is an anthology or reader in mission. You will find various perspectives from professors, missiologists, and other writers, who share their insights concerning the nature, history and new possibilities for mission. An anthology never reads like a novel. Rather, it is more like an a la carte menu from which you may choose to linger over the tastiest morsels.

My thanks to the many authors who allowed us to share in their witness.

I am convinced that we need not fear the future, "for God has not given us a spirit of fear, but a spirit of power and love and a sound mind." (2 Timothy 1:7, J. B. Phillips)

Acknowledgments

Wilbert R. Shenk, "The Transfiguration of Mission," is excerpted from *The Transfiguration of Mission: Biblical, Theological, and Historical Foundations* edited by Wilbert R. Shenk, copyright 1993. Used with permission of Herald Press, Scottdale, PA, all rights reserved.

Darrell L. Guder, "From Sending to Being Sent," is excerpted from *Missional Church: A Vision for the Sending of the Church in North America* edited by Darrel L. Guder (1998); Lesslie Newbigin, "The Pattern of the Christian World Mission," "A Changed Context," and "Mission Evangelism in Secular Societies," are excerpted from *A Word in Season* by Lesslie Newbigin (1994); Donald R. Jacobs, "Contextualization in Mission," is excerpted from *Toward the 21st Century in Christian Mission* edited by James M. Phillips and Robert M. Coote (1993); Andrew F. Walls, "The North American Context," is excerpted from "The American Dimension of the Missionary Movement" in *Earthen Vessels: American Evangelicals and Foreign Missions, 1880-1980* edited by Joel A. Carpenter and Wilbert R. Shenk (1990), all published by Wm. B. Eerdmans Publishing, Grand Rapids, MI. Used with permission of the publisher.

Ronald E. Osborn, "Missionary," is excerpted from *Creative Disarray: Models of Ministry in a Changing America* by Ronald E. Osborn (St. Louis: Chalice Press, 1991). Used with permission of Chalice Press.

Dana L. Robert, "American Women in Mission," is excerpted from *American Women in Mission: A Social History of Their Thought and Practice* by Dana L. Robert (Macon, GA: Mercer University Press, 1996). Used with permission of the publisher.

The excerpts from Glory E. Dharmaraj, Samuel Escobar, and Edward W. Poitras, are taken, respectively, from "Women as Border-Crossing Agents: Transforming the Center from the Margins" by Glory E. Dharmaraj in *Missiology*, 26, 1 (January 1998): 55-66; "Mission from the Margins to the Margins: Two Case Studies from Latin America" by Samuel Escobar in *Missiology*, 26, 1 (January 1998): 87-95; and "Joy in Receiving: A Reflection on Mission Motive and Modality" by Edward W. Poitras in *Missiology*, 23, 4 (October 1995): 387-399. All are used with permission of *Missiology: An International Review*.

Joan Delaney, "Recruitment of Protestant Missionaries," is excerpted from *A Comparative Study of Christian Mission* by Joan Delaney (U.S. Catholic Mission Association, 1998), pp. 13-14, and is used with permission of the U.S. Catholic Mission Association.

Thomas H. Graves and Alan Neely, "Case Study: Singing the Lord's Song," is excerpted from *Christian Mission: A Case Study Approach* by Alan Neely (Maryknoll, NY: Orbis, 1995), pp. 186-90, copyright © 1995 Orbis Books. Used with permission.

Alan Neely, "What Is a Context?" is excerpted from "What Is a Context and What Is Contextualization?" in *Christian Mission: A Case Study Approach* by Alan Neely (Maryknoll, NY: Orbis, 1995), pp. 3-4, 8-9, copyright © 1995 Orbis Books. Used with permission.

Alan Neely, "Case Study: 'What's the Matter, Abdaraman?'" is excerpted from *Christian Mission: A Case Study Approach* by Alan Neely (Maryknoll, NY: Orbis, 1995), pp. 78-81, and adapted from Carlo Carretto's book *Letters from the Desert* (Maryknoll, NY: Orbis, 1972), copyright © 1972 Orbis Books. Used with permission.

Alan Neely, "An Approach to Case Studies," in the Teacher's Guide, is excerpted from *Christian Mission: A Case Study Approach* by Alan Neely (Maryknoll, N.Y.: Orbis, 1995), pp. 13-19, copyright © 1995 Orbis Books. Used with permission.

Stan Skreslet, "Emerging Trends in Context," "Islam: A Major Factor for the 21st Century," and "Economic Refugees," are excerpted from "Emerging Trends in a Shifting Global Context: Mission in the New World Order" by Stan Skreslet in *Theology Today* (July 1997): 150-164, and are used with permission of *Theology Today*.

Mercy Amba Oduyoye, "The Church of the Future: A View from Africa," is excerpted from "The Church and the Future, Its Mission and Theology: A View from Africa" by Mercy Amba Oduyoye in *Theology Today* (January 1996): 494-505, and is used with permission of *Theology Today*.

Jonathan Kozol, "Amazing Grace," is excerpted from *Amazing Grace* by Jonathan Kozol, copyright © 1995 by Jonathan Kozol. Used with permission of Crown Publishers, Inc.

M. Thomas Thangaraj, "Relating to People of Other Religions," is excerpted from *Relating to People of Other Religions: What Every Christian Needs to Know* by M. Thomas Thangaraj (Nashville: Abingdon Press, 1997), pp. 7-8, 31-35, 101-7, copyright © 1997 Abingdon Press. Used with permission.

Harold J. Recinos, "Who Comes in the Name of the Lord?" is excerpted from *Who Comes in the Name of the Lord?* by Harold J. Recinos (Nashville: Abingdon Press, 1997), pp. 19-33, 143-55, copyright © 1997 Abingdon Press. Used with permission.

Howard Snyder, "Earthcurrents," is excerpted from *EarthCurrents: The Struggle for the World's Soul* by Howard Snyder (Nashville: Abingdon Press, 1995), pp. 75-77, 177-85, 242-46, copyright © 1995 Abingdon Press. Used with permission.

Donald E. Messer, "No Nonpersons in God's Family," is excerpted from *A Conspiracy of Goodness: Contemporary Images of Christian Mission* by Donald E. Messer (Nashville: Abingdon Press, 1992), pp. 91-108, copyright © 1992 Abingdon Press. Used with permission.

Sara Bhattacharji, "Challenges in the Context of Globalization," is excepted from "Mission 2000: An Agenda" in *International Review of Mission*, LXXXVI, 343 (October 1997): 399-401. Used with permission of *International Review of Mission*.

William Fore, "Communication and Human Dignity," is excerpted from *Church & Society* (November/December 1997): 37-46, with permission of the Presbyterian Church (USA).

Gladys McCue Taylor and Gladys Taylor Cook, "Bridges in Spirituality," is excerpted from *Bridges in Spirituality: First Nations Christian Women Tell Their Stories* edited by Joyce Carlson and Alf Dumont (Toronto: United Church Publishing House, 1997), pp. 73, 90, 103, 132-33, 140. Used with permission of the United Church Publishing House.

M. L. Daneel, "Earthkeeping," is excerpted from "Earthkeeping in Missiological Perspective: An African

Challenge" by M. L. Daneel in *Mission Studies*, XIII, 1-2 (1996): 25-26. Used with permission of *Mission Studies*.

Ngoy Mulunda-Nyanga, "Forgiveness and Reconciliation," is excerpted from *The Reconstruction of Africa: Faith and Freedom for a Conflicted Continent* by Ngoy Mulunda-Nyanga (Nairobi, Kenya: All Africa Conference of Churches, 1997), pp. 59-84, 126, with the permission of the author.

Mary Previte, "The Shape of Your Mountain," is excerpted from *Children and Violence: The Washington Forum Perspectives on Our Global Future* by Mary Previte, copyright © 1997 World Vision Inc. Used with permission.

Tex Sample, "Learning by Apprenticeship," is reproduced from *Ministry in an Oral Culture: Living with Will Rogers, Uncle Remus and Minnie Pearl* by Tex Sample, copyright © 1994 Tex Sample. Used with permission of Westminster John Knox Press.

Garnett E. Foster, "Case Study: 'A Church for All People?'" is excerpted from *Journal for Case Teaching*, 5 (Fall 1993): 95-97, copyright © Case Study Institute. Used with permission. All names have been disguised to protect the privacy of the individuals involved.

The maps "The World by Population" and "The World by Income" are adapted from maps of those titles appearing in *Mission Handbook, 1998 =2000* edited by John A. Siewert and Edna G. Valdez, copyright © 1997 MARC Publications, a division of World Vision International. Used with permission of World Vision International.

The charts "Christianity and Islam: The Ebb and Flow," and "The Christian Church Grows Serially," are adapted from charts with those titles in *Mission Handbook, 1998-2000* edited by John A. Siewert and Edna G. Valdez, copyright © 1997 MARC Publications, a division of World Vision International. Used with permission of World Vision International.

1. Eve of a New Millennium

Introduction

Do all the good you can,
By all the means you can,
In all the ways you can,
In all the places you can,
At all the times you can,
To all the people you can,
As long as ever you can.
—John Wesley

The first task in charting mission for the future is to take account of where we are and where we want to be. Picture a map:

If we do not know where we want to go, we should remember the character in *Alice in Wonderland* who said, "If you don't know where you want to go, it doesn't matter which path you take." Knowing where we have been helps to orient us and names the gifts, experiences and insights we have to take with us.

In this chapter we encounter some of the biblical mandates for mission; then Wilbert Shenk helps us understand that the last two hundred years of mission, commonly called the "Modern Mission Movement" is only one-tenth of our history in the Christian church. He also explains that a relevant mission is always en route. Darrell Guder reminds us that the North American church is shaped by nations who understood Christianity as their state religion, even in countries such as the United States where it is by culture and not law. Bishop Emilio De Carvalho illustrates the changing nature of mission by describing the transformation of mission in Angola.

Once when Vihn Tran, a pastor of Vietnamese origin, was a vice-chair of the former

Mission Education and Cultivation Department of the General Board of Global Ministries, it fell to him to preside over a meeting. He was very nervous; he felt new to the English language and especially new to Robert's Rules of Order. The time came for the first vote. He asked all who were in favor to say "Yes." There was a resounding "Yes." Then he asked for the next subject. I gently reminded him that he must ask for the "no" votes, as well. He looked surprised and said, "With mission, there is only 'Yes!'

In a similar way, Guder reminds us that mission is not a program to be voted upon. It is the very nature of the church.

Called into God's Mission
Rena M. Yocom

Many persons are surprised that the word "mission" is not in the Bible. How is it that mission can be so central to the nature of the church if it is not to be found in Scripture? The answer is simple. The word "mission" comes from a Latin word that refers to the particular task or assignment given to a person sent on another's behalf. Therefore, one can read about military persons who have been sent on a particular mission. More recently, advertising and managing experts have suggested that every business must be able to state its mission. Such a mission statement is posted and distributed so that every employee knows what is expected and required.

Where do we turn to find our mission statement? Obviously, we turn to Scripture.

"Go therefore and make disciples"
   (Matthew 28:19-20)
Sending out the disciples two by two (Mark 6:7-13)
Women at the empty tomb (Luke 24:1-11)
Samaritan woman at the well (John 4)
Disciples as witnesses to the ends of the earth
   (Acts 1:8)
"Come over to Macedonia" (Paul's vision)
   (Acts 16:9-10)
"Just as you did it to the least of these"
   (Matthew 25:31-46)
Healing of demoniac and woman (Mark 5:1-34)
Parable of Good Samaritan (Luke 10:30-37)

"Feed my sheep" (John 21:15-19)
"What I have I give you" (Acts 3:6)
Good news to the poor, release to the captives
   (Luke 4:18)
"Let justice roll down like waters"
   (Amos 5:24)
Swords into plowshares (Micah 4:3)
"What does the Lord require?" (Micah 6:8)
Varieties of gifts, one body in Christ
   (1 Corinthians 12)
Many gifts, one spirit (Ephesians 4:1-16)
"Love one another" (1 John 3:11)

United Methodists share with other Christians the conviction that Scripture is the primary source and criterion for Christian doctrine. As we open our minds and hearts to the Word of God, faith is born and nourished, our understanding is deepened, and the possibilities for transforming the world become apparent to us. (The Book of Discipline of The United Methodist Church, 1996, para. 63)

There are many biblical passages that inform us of our mission, of what we are to do on God's behalf as we are sent into the world. The following is a representative list; it is not exhaustive nor exclusive.

If these are at the heart of our biblical mandate for mission (understanding that other passages could be added), we can begin to see a pattern in the particular work or assignments that go with these verses. As one looks at these tasks of mission, there are four primary types or forms for the mission we do in Christ's name. The same Spirit shapes them all.

Passage   **Task(s)**

Form I: Proclamation and Witness

Passage	Task(s)
Mark 6:7-13	Go (without money), proclaim repentance
Luke 24:1-11	Go, tell others of risen Christ
John 4	Evangelize, testify to our experience, bring others to Christ
Acts 1:8	Receive power of Holy Spirit, witness to the risen Christ at home, next door, and around the world
Acts 16:9-10	Listen to God, cross borders, proclaim Christ

Form II: Tending the Needs of Humanity

Passage	Task(s)
Matthew 25:31-46	Feed the hungry, give drink to the thirsty, welcome the stranger, clothe the naked, care for the sick, visit the prisoners, see Christ in persons society discounts
Mark 5:1-34	Heal the afflicted, cast out demons, touch the untouchables
Luke 10:30-37	Show mercy, care for the injured, care for perceived "enemies," bind wounds, give of your own money, care for those who cannot repay you, do more than society requires
John 21:15-19	Feed the hungry, tend the followers of Jesus
Acts 3:6	Give what you have—the power of Christ, heal the lame

Form III: Advocating for Change in Systems That Oppress

Passage	Task(s)
Luke 4:18	Minister/bring good news to the poor, proclaim release for prisoners and sight for the blind, advocate for and free the oppressed

Amos 5:24	Work for justice, change unjust systems
Micah 4:3	Advocate for peace and reconciliation
Micah 6:8	Do justice, be kind, be humble

Form IV: Reciprocal and Reconciling Ministries

1 Corinthians 12	Need one another, appreciate gifts for the good of all
Ephesians 4:1-16	Be gentle and patient, be one in spirit, be peacemakers
1 John 3:11	Love one another, even give life for one another, love in action and not just words

Unfortunately, in the church there is a tendency to debate which of these missional efforts is the most important. Sometimes people argue that the first focus is the real mission, that the second focus is "humanitarian aid" and that the third focus is "meddling." The basis for such claims is nebulous since all of these come from God's written word to us.

As Paul clarifies in his letter to the church at Corinth, God has given to each individual and each community of faith unique gifts. Praise God! Nevertheless, these gifts were all given for the common good (1 Corinthians 12:7). Therefore, we can know that God, in his infinite wisdom, has gifted persons and congregations within the church to accomplish all the forms of the mission that must be accomplished in Christ's name.

Because of their unique gifts, individuals and congregations may want to participate most fully in a particular form of mission. That is to be celebrated! Yet corporately, as a denomination, as the expression of United Methodism in a particular geographical area, we must see that all forms of mission are expressed, lest some child of God be lost or forgotten along the margins of our society.

The most vivid portraits for the last two hundred years have focused on the first two forms of mission. No one would challenge the impact of the ministry of Billy Graham or Mother Teresa. The risk for the churches in North America is that we view ourselves as giving out of our "plenty" and therefore without need. If our only self-perception is as giver or sender, we begin to make decisions about God's mission as though it were a Christmas gift or card list. We scratch off the name of any recipient who has not responded with gratitude to our initiatives.

Recently, I was at a United Methodist gathering in which some expressed indignation that missionaries from other countries were coming to the United States. One person asked, "Why don't they go where they are needed?" Perhaps they did. On the eve of this new millennium, Christians must live out their calling and gifts for mission, regardless of their earthly citizenship.

We are sent on a mission—God's mission. It has multiple forms, but it is not a multiple choice quiz. All of these missional mandates are based in Scripture. Let the church respond with Isaiah: "Here am I; send me!"

The Transfiguration of Mission

Wilbert R. Shenk, Professor of Mission History and Contemporary Culture, Fuller Theological Seminary, Pasadena, California

Excerpted from *The Transfiguration of Mission: Biblical, Theological, and Historical Foundations*, ed. Wilbert R. Shenk (Scottdale, Pa.: Herald Press, 1993), 17-36.

Mission denotes action: being sent with a commission to perform a certain task, acting in the name of a superior, carrying out an important mandate, serving as ambassador on behalf of one's leader. It is not a specifically religious term. It is used by military, government, business, and many other secular groups.

Missiology is the formal study of the Christian mission, including the biblical and theological foundation of mission; the history of the course taken by the missions; analysis of the contemporary context; and a discernment of social, political, economic, and religious trends that will influence the direction of mission in the future.

. . . .

The Modern Mission Movement

Symbolically, modern missions may be dated from 1792 when the English Baptist cobbler-preacher, William Carey, published *An Enquiry into the Obligation of Christians to Use Means for the Conversion of the Heathens* and, prodded by Carey and his sympathizers, the Baptists founded a missionary society that same year. Over the next thirty years, many other groups in Great Britain, Europe, and North America would emulate this step. This set a pattern that continued to be followed by one group after another throughout the next two hundred years.

Two centuries later we can say, quite simply, that this movement has changed the face of the Christian church worldwide. In 1800, seven years after the Carey family had arrived in India, an estimated 86 percent of all Christians in the world were white Europeans. By 2000 at least 60 percent of all Christians will be found in Asia, Africa, and Latin America. . . . The implications of this historical shift are still not widely understood and appreciated by Christians in the West. Its meaning will become inescapably clearer as we move into the twenty-first century.

The modern mission movement has come in for its share of criticism from those within the family of faith who are members of churches that are themselves the fruit of missions. This group asserts that the church in the West, including Western missions, has compromised them and the Christian message by an uncritical hand-in-glove alliance with Western political, economic, and military power.

A Relevant Missiology

A relevant missiology will be one that brings the fullness of biblical revelation in Jesus the Messiah to bear on the mission task as it is unfolding before us. The burden of this work has been to ask what this implies for faithful discipleship.

The frontiers of mission in the twenty-first century will be markedly different from those of the past two hundred years. The church, more widely dispersed than ever before, will be in a minority position in most countries with the specter of persecution always hovering over some part of the messianic community somewhere. . . .

A relevant missiology will be one that helps the church embrace its mission fully through a clear discernment of the times, together with a vision of what a dynamic missionary response requires. The church must maintain an awareness that faithfulness, both to its own nature and to its responsibility to the world, requires a stance of missionary encounter.

. . . .

One searches the Scriptures in vain for any discussion or description of mission strategy. But there is a consistent thread running throughout the story of "calling and sending," beginning with Abraham and continuing with Jesus and the early church. It is to be seen most fully in Jesus. In Jesus the Messiah, God takes on human form, identifying fully with the objects of his love. . . .

Yet standing over the incarnation there is always the cross and atonement. The incarnation signifies total vulnerability and expendability, including the risk of crucifixion. The fundamental missionary stance is that of the servant. The strategy is the incarnation. The sign marking the way of mission is the cross. . . .

A relevant missiology will be based on the work of Jesus the Messiah. It will always be missiology en route. It is not a set of timeless axioms waiting to be applied in all situations. Rather it will be a dynamic missiology to the degree it is continually tested and applied as the messianic community witnesses to the world of its own experience of being transformed through encounter with the Messiah.

Missional Church: From Sending to Being Sent

Darrell L. Guder, Professor of Evangelism and Church Growth, Columbia Theological Seminary, Decatur, Georgia

Excerpted from *Missional Church: A Vision for the Sending of the Church in North America,* ed. Darrell L. Guder (Grand Rapids: Eerdmans, 1998), 1-7.

As we move toward the end of the century, more and more commentators are pro-

Changing paradigms of mission thinking

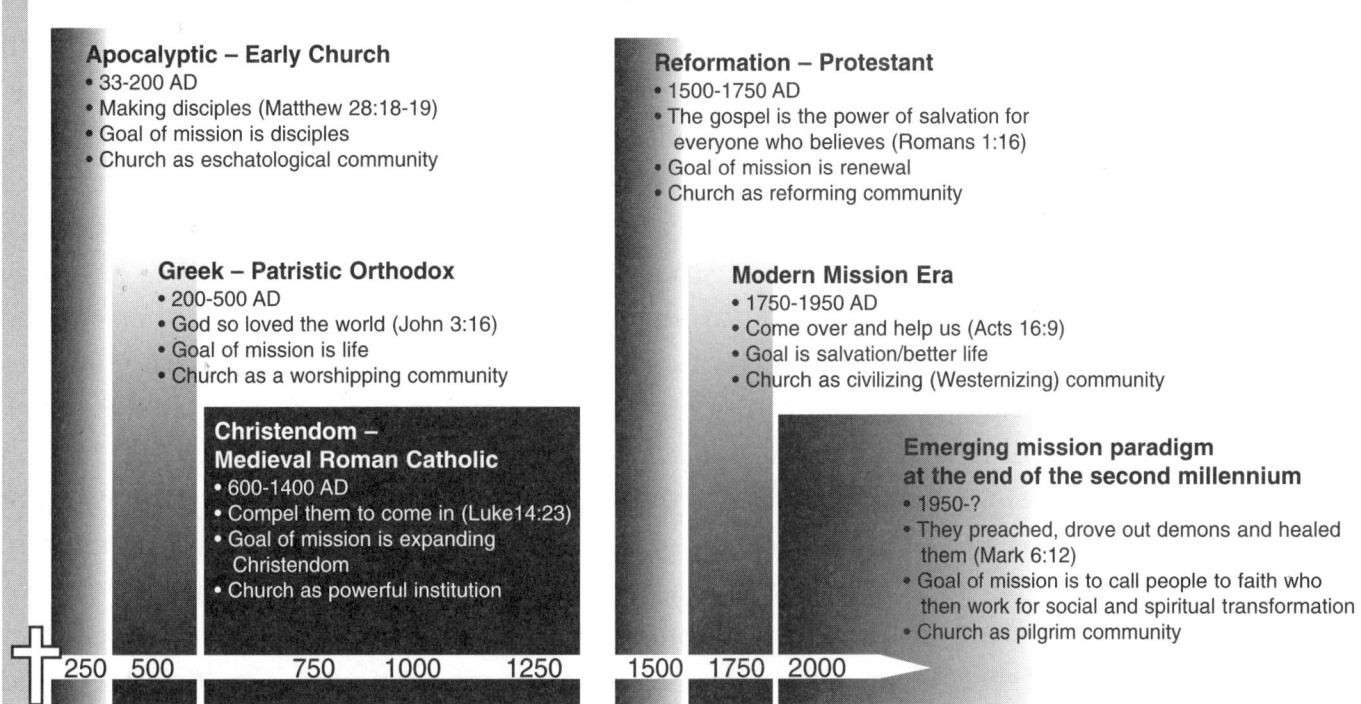

Adapted from Bosch, *Transforming Mission* (Orbis, 1991) from World Vision in *1998-2000 Mission Handbook*.

posing their versions of the "great new fact of our time." Among the many great new facts suggested, Christians in North America would likely point to two. On the one hand, during the twentieth century Christianity has become a truly worldwide movement, with churches established on every continent and among every major cultural group. The great modern missionary movement has been, despite all the controversy and debate, a truly successful enterprise. On the other hand, Christianity in North America has moved (or been moved) away from its position of dominance as it has experienced the loss not only of numbers but of power and influence within society.

The United States is still, by all accounts, a very religious society. The pollsters affirm that Americans and Canadians believe in God, pray regularly, and consider themselves religious. But they find less and less reason to express their faith by joining a Christian church. North American religiosity is changing profoundly by becoming more pluralistic, more individualistic, and more private. . . . Rather than occupying a central and influential place, North American Christian churches are increasingly marginalized, so much so that in our urban areas they represent a minority movement. It is by now a truism to speak of North America as a mission field.

Neither the structures nor the theology of our established Western traditional churches is missional. They are shaped by the legacy of Christendom. That is, they have been formed by centuries in which Western civilization considered itself formally and officially Christian. . . .Even when the legal structures of Christendom have been removed (as in North America), the legacy continues as a pattern of powerful traditions, attitudes, and social structures that we describe as "functional Christendom."

In the approach of Christendom, mission became only one of the many programs of the church. Mission boards emerged in Western churches to do the work of foreign mission. Yet even here the Western churches understood themselves as sending churches, and they assumed the destination of their sending to be the pagan reaches of the world that needed both the gospel and "the benefits of Western civilization." In like manner, Western churches also developed home mission or inner mission, as the emerging secularism of Western societies presented us with new challenges. But it has taken us decades to realize that mission is not just a program of the church. It defines the church as God's sent people. Either we are defined by mission, or we reduce the scope of the gospel and the mandate of the church. Thus our challenge today is to move from church with mission to missional church.

Congregations still tend to view missions as one of several programs of the church. Evangelism, when present, is usually defined as member recruitment at the local level and as church planting at the regional level. The sending-receiving mentality is still strong as churches collect funds and send them off to genuine mission enterprises elsewhere. Indeed, the main business of many mission committees is to determine how to spend the mission budget rather than view the entire congregational budget as an exercise in mission.

As denominational and centralized structures diminish in importance and power, local congregations are beginning to see their own context as their mission. But even with that shift, few have taken the necessary steps to redefine themselves as missionary by their very nature.

. . . .

What would an understanding of the church look like if it were truly missional in design and definition?

The Transformational Role of the Church in Angola

Bishop Emilio J. M. De Carvalho, Bishop, Western Angola Area, Luanda, Angola, Africa

Excerpted from "The Transformational Role of the Church in Post-Liberation Angola," in *Mission and Transformation in a Changing World* (New York: General Board of Global Ministries, 1998), 47-48.

The mission of the church, analyzed historically, has changed to adapt itself to the nuances of our national histories.

When the first foreign missionaries came to Angola at the end of the nineteenth century, they saw us as a people in need of the gospel, so they prioritized preaching. They saw us deeply immersed in ignorance, so they opened schools. They saw us afflicted by many diseases, so they opened hospitals in the inland parts of the country. Their mission was to save us from sin, ignorance, and death.

Later on, as oppressive regimes tried to keep us backward, the mission of the church also became a struggle to liberate us from slavery and oppression. It helped us to attain and affirm our identity as peoples, thus freeing us from systems of division and alienation.

In the last twenty years, however, the picture has dramatically changed!

The forces of evil, not happy that through much pain and sacrifice we managed some achievements, pushed us into devastating wars. These have been going on throughout the continent for the last two decades, fueling new regional conflicts and substantially changing the traditional mission of the church.

The consequences of such wars (which are not cold wars, tribal wars, or civil wars, since they involve mercenaries from foreign lands) can be seen in Angola:

- fragmentation of our human values, family ties, and unity as a people;
- alienation from our cultural, ethical, and religious values;
- exposure of our children to the horror and shame of war;
- thousands of human beings killed or left homeless, displaced, handicapped, poor, hungry, or forced to become refugees;
- destruction of most of the educational and economic structures of the country;
- the seeding of violence, hatred, and death;
- turning love and understanding into political and ideological confrontation;
- the presence of thousands of land mines that continue to claim lives, mostly of women and children;
- the vulnerability of a wealthy country to national and international investors and exploiters thirsty for easy gain;
- increasing drug traffic, drug abuse, violations of women's rights, and sexual exploitation that even extends to children under eighteen.

- under the umbrella of democracy, the spread of fundamentalist churches and sects, most of which are undefined as far as theological and ethical concepts are concerned.

How should the church be in mission in such a society?

The transformational role of the church must be to change a culture of war and violence into a culture of justice, peace, and reconciliation. It must give back to the forsaken Africa populations the values that they have lost during years of wars and of disregard for one another. It must move us from where we stand to where African Christians believe God is calling us to be: on the frontier.

. . . .

The church must uncover new ways of extending its witness and mission and *be* the church to the suffering peoples of our world by sharing its resources, its spiritual life, and its love with them. These are new times. We must simply refuse to drink old wine from old wineskins. The mission of The United Methodist Church in these new times must be to transform a culture of violence and war into a culture of peace, love, justice, and reconciliation.

A mighty task indeed.

2. The Sent People of God

Introduction

In 1963, Tracey Jones (then head of the Division of World Missions, later the general secretary of the General Board of Global Ministries) wrote a book entitled *Our Mission Today*. In it he said the following:

> We have seen that the 19th century missionary movement, one of the most creative in the entire history of the Church, was characterized by four images:
> 1. *The mission field*, seen as . . . villages that had never heard the gospel;
> 2. The *missionary*, seen as a white man who went to a distant land. . . ;
> 3. The word *liberation* meant westernizing Asians, Africans . . . for Christianity and Western culture were identified as two sides of the same coin.
> 4. The restless *explorer* seen as the pioneer . . . who could not be quieted until every geographical barrier had been crossed.
>
> . . . It should be no surprise . . . to find that these images of the last century have lost their capacity to define our situation and to elicit a response from thoughtful men and women struggling with a complex technological age. . . . The fundamental nature of the mission as God's offer of reconciliation through Jesus Christ does not change, but our ways of expressing it in word, deed, and organization do change.[1]

In this section, readers, with the assistance of Ronald Osborn and Dana Robert, will relive the passion of another era for the role and symbolic nature of the office of missionary. Dana Robert and Glory Dharmaraj help us appreciate the unique contributions of women in mission leadership. Lesslie Newbigin reminds us how the movement of the last two centuries followed the pattern and flow of world powers, and how, with the success of that missionary movement, the center for Christianity in the new century will shift to the south.

The case study and Donald Jacobs' article on contextualization free us to look at mission through the eyes of those who have received the gospel. They challenge us to ask, Does God speak only in European languages? Must Christians dress like North Americans? Since Wesley used tunes from the London pubs, might missionaries today use melodies, rhythms, and instruments from their cultures?

As United Methodists we can celebrate the increase of indigenous leadership around the globe. It gives a new depth and breadth to the leadership of the denomination. We also know that the church in any place is not dependent on "outside" leadership. Even when God's witnesses from other nations are asked to leave, the church is still present and vital.

Missionary

Ronald E. Osborn, retired from teaching positions at School of Theology at Claremont, California, with other teaching experiences at Union Theological Seminary in the Philippines and The Ecumenical Institute, Chateau de Bossey, Switzerland

Excerpted from *Creative Disarray: Models of Ministry in a Changing America* (St. Louis: Chalice Press, 1991), 105-13.

The nineteenth-century form of saint was the missionary. The concept arose in a world of perception and sentiment so radically different from our own that anyone born after 1940 can scarcely conceive its energizing power and emotional pull on the life of the churches while it flourished during "The Great Century" of foreign missions.

The marks of holiness showed as clearly upon the missionary as ever upon any saint. The great commission to go into all the world had come as a divine call personally addressed to each young woman or man who volunteered for this ministry, whether the voice of God was heard in ecstasy actually sounding out one's name and guiding to Burma or China or Africa, or, as was more often the case, the reading of a particular scripture seized one as unmistakably as if a letter with one's name on it had just fallen from heaven.

The sacrifice necessitated by the missionary's spending years on end among an alien people of strange speech and custom—exposed to diseases and hostility and danger to life, cut off from home and family and one's own kind, tested by endless months of fruitless witness before one convert could be claimed and by the outspoken doubts of critics at home—marked this minister with a holiness as patently genuine as that bestowed by any shaman's ecstatic vision.

Especially touching to the Age of Romanticism was the recurring departure of the missionary, after a brief furlough in the homeland to recruit one's strength and spirits and to inform the churches of the work. The evident eagerness to return to the task, the firm renunciation of enticements and attachments so dear to the sentimental heart of the time, the resolute faithfulness to the divine call, the willingness to be separated even from one's children—all gave evidence of a level of devotion at which ordinary pastors and church members could only marvel.

. . . .

The dramatic surge of missionary zeal and activity in the nineteenth century provides a stirring chapter in the history of the church. . . . In the young American nation, knowledge of the great world elsewhere heightened awareness of strange peoples in "heathen" nations. The thought of millions living and dying in darkness, without the light of the gospel, stirred Christian hearts. . . .

By the end of the century Christian graduates streamed from the campuses every year to offer themselves for service, as the student volunteer movement gained momentum. . . . The tide continued to rise until the Great Depression of the 1930s, and only after World War II did it dramatically slacken in the mainline churches as the Christian movement in the far fields came to maturity and indigenous leaders assumed the leadership in evangelization and teaching.

When the great migration of missionaries was at its peak, few other Americans had even crossed the Atlantic, much less the Pacific, and sea mail was the most rapid form of communication with home. Every denomination had its missionary society or board, with a remarkably well organized root-system reaching into the congregations for nourishment by their gifts and prayers.

Scores of hymns written and sung in those times catch up the excitement, the fervid hopes, and the dedication exemplified by the missionary, but expected in every good Christian:

> If you cannot cross the ocean,
> And the heathen lands explore,
> You can find the heathen nearer,
> You can help them at your door;
> If you cannot give your thousands,
> You can give the widow's mite,
> And the least you give for Jesus
> Will be precious in his sight.[2]

Alongside foreign missions, the movement for home missions grew apace. In response to a widely circulated story about a party of Flathead and Nez Percé Indians who had made their way from the headwaters of the Missouri down to St. Louis to ask for "the white man's Book of Heaven," Methodist Jason Lee set out for the Northwest in 1834.

. . . .

The work in home missions broadened to launch Protestant efforts among the Hispanics in the newly acquired Southwest. These people were of course already Christians, but the institutions of Catholicism were weak and Protestants deemed that faith inadequate for freedom-loving Americans. . . .

Home missions boards sponsored educational efforts among the newly freed blacks after the Civil War, but it was hardly necessary to establish churches, given the effectiveness of the black preachers already on the scene.

As the flood of immigration mounted, effort turned toward the evangelization and Americanization of the millions of newcomers. For many their entry into a strange pattern of life was eased a bit, and some found their way into Protestant churches.

The home missionary enterprise was much broader in scope than can be suggested here. Less exotic than the overseas venture, it arose from the same impulses, flourished in the same environment, and appealed, if with slightly less emotional power, to the same sense of the romantic. The sacrificial image of the missionary overshadowed the total effort.

The ministry of the missionary was monopolized less by white males than any other nineteenth-century form of ministry. Young African Americans of unusual ability returned to the lands of their ancestors in the service of the gospel. Several Indian American preachers received tiny allowances from boards of home missions to support their ministry among the tribal peoples, as did a few Hispanic Protestant preachers to labor among their own in the Southwest. When work was undertaken among Asian immigrants on the Pacific coast, a preacher of Chinese or Japanese or Filipino descent was occasionally found.

Most notable was the service of women in the vocation of missionary. Under leading Protestant boards, both husband and wife received an appointment and stipend, both had responsibilities, and both were set apart for the task in moving services of dedication. In addition to wives, numbers of unmarried women also entered this ministry. Bible-quoting adherents of patriarchy in the churches at home seemed untroubled about sending women to teach the heathen.

. . . .

The missionary believed wholeheartedly in the power of the gospel to save and in the obligation to make that gospel known. All this had been revealed by God in Holy Scripture. One of the chief tasks of the missionary pioneers, therefore, was to translate the Bible into the languages of the many peoples to whom they had come. . . .

With rare exceptions, the early missionaries saw their faith and their culture as of a piece: To offer one was to offer the other. Those who went from the United States also assumed that their nation, committed to the holy cause of freedom, represented the fullest flower of Christian civilization. Thus they commended along with the gospel the political concepts and the heroes of their people. The nation was young and hopeful. Cynicism was not yet a conditioned reflex. And many Americans, including the missionaries, loved this land with a pure and simple devotion. . . .

The compassion of the missionaries, along with their belief that modern knowledge could reduce the miseries they saw on every hand, moved them to address a broad range of human need. They preached the gospel in every way they could. They also started hospitals, clinics, orphanages, schools, colleges, printing establishments, projects in translation, agricultural experimental stations, light industries, and every other constructive venture they could imagine and manage.

. . . .

The fruition of the missionary venture came in the emergence of indigenous leadership and the independence of the "younger churches" . . . In the twentieth century, indigenous leaders have assumed increasing responsibility for ministry in congregational and general church life and for administration of hospitals, schools, and other institutions, the ownership of which has passed to the new churches themselves.

Among many so-called evangelical and conservative bodies, however, older paternalistic patterns persist with force unabated, as do the cultural and theological assumptions from which they derived. But in the life of the mainline Protestant churches the missionary is a specialist with a rare and needed skill invited by the church overseas for a term as a fraternal worker.

But the notion of ministry as self-denying has not died. It clings to the conscience of many a minister, so that we feel downright uneasy about the display of obvious luxury. To such an extent, the model of the missionary has preserved the memory of the apostolic ministry which enriched the life of the world.

American Women in Mission

Dana L. Robert, Professor of International Mission, Boston University School of Theology, Boston, Massachusetts

Excerpted from *American Women in Mission: A Social History of Their Thought and Practice* (Macon, Ga.: Mercer University Press, 1996), 125-30, 409-18.

Help Those Women

Those
Those who alone in Christ Jesus now glory,
Saved by His power from the thraldom of sin,
Joyfully telling redemption's glad story,
Hastening their sisters from bondage to win.
Sisters no less, though in deep degradation,
Shrouded in darkness, they helplessly fall.
Sisters? Ah, yes, we confess the relation,
Since our Elder Brother acknowledges all.
Help those who labor to rescue and save them,
Lifting them up from the mire and the clay,
Breaking the customs that long have enslaved them,
Cheering their hearts with the gospel's bright ray.

Women

Women who lingered near Calvary weeping,
Last at the cross when all others had fled,
First at His grave, where the angels were keeping
Watch o'er the tomb of Immanuel dead.
Dead? Nay. "Why seek ye the dead 'mong the living?
Jesus is risen!" the angels proclaim.
Go teach all nations, eternal life giving
Freely to all who believe in His name.
Haste till the ends of the earth are awaking,
Shout, as on love's swiftest pinions ye flee.
Watchman in Zion, behold the light breaking!
Help now those women who labor with thee!

—Mary Sparkes Wheeler, *Heathen Woman's Friend*, February 1879

In 1854, the Scottish missionary Alexander Duff, advocate of mission schools and English-language education, visited the General Conference of the Methodist Episcopal Church. Addressing the highest governmental body of the largest Protestant denomination in America, Duff appealed for American Methodists to open mission work in India....

In 1856, the Reverend William Butler, his wife Clementina, and their four children caught a steamer for India. They were Irish Wesleyans who had immigrated to the United States. After serving some years in local parishes, Butler felt called to open the India mission for the American Methodists.... Shocked at seeing the bodies of abandoned women floating in the Ganges, Clementina Butler realized that missionary women needed to help Indian women improve their condition in society.

When the Sepoy Rebellion began in 1857, the Butlers fled for their lives and were under siege for eight months. The first female convert of the fledgling mission, Miss Maria Bolst, was beheaded by the Sepoys who targeted native converts as stooges of the imperialist government. The lives of the Butlers were saved by the British, who crushed the rebellion and executed its leaders. Reassessing his mission priorities in light of the rebellion, Butler received a "glorious vision" that he should take in girls orphaned during the uprising and that Methodist women should organize to educate the orphans....

At the time that American Methodists organized their denominational mission board in 1819, Methodist women in New York City founded their own auxiliary that helped to outfit and to support the single women who went out before mid-century. The New York Female Missionary Society of the Methodist Episcopal Church was thus the main supporter of Ann Wilkins, pioneer missionary in Liberia. Another Methodist women's organization that raised money to support single women was the Ladies' China Missionary Society, organized by Methodist women in Baltimore, Maryland. . . .

After nine years in the field, the Butlers received a well-deserved furlough when they were appointed to a local church in Chelsea, Massachusetts. At the same time, a group of women in the Boston area became convinced that women across the country needed to organize themselves to meet the needs of women around the world—women whose segregation from men in places such as China and India meant that only female missionaries could evangelize them. . . . Mrs. Butler and Mrs. Winslow, a Congregationalist missionary wife, described "the degradation and woes of heathen women," and emphasized that single women could give themselves completely to the needs of indigenous women.[3] Their ecumenical attempts thwarted by continued denominational objection, the women soon reconstituted themselves as the Woman's Board of Missions. The three goals of the Woman's Board were to work for women and children through the American Board, to increase knowledge of missions among women, and to train children into mission work.[4]

The Woman's Foreign Missionary Society of the Methodist Episcopal Church was the second to organize, with the help of the indefatigable Mrs. Butler. Clergy opposed the women's desires to work ecumenically, and the model for women's work became denominational at the insistence of men who feared the funneling of money and power away from their own denomination. . . . Despite clerical suspicion, women held mission "union meetings" throughout the late nineteenth century.

Hearing of the new women's mission boards, missionary wives in the field poured out their hearts to female correspondents at home, requesting that they organize themselves for mission work to women. . . . By 1900, over forty denominational women's societies existed, with three million active women, some despite sustained hostility from the men of the church.[5] Publicizing projects through their mission magazines, women in local church auxiliaries nickeled and dimed their way into building hospitals and schools around the world, paying the salaries of indigenous female evangelists, and sending single women as missionary doctors, teachers, and evangelists.

The secret to the provenance of the woman's missionary movement across the United States was the unity among married and single women, prominent and ordinary women, missionary and homeside women, and women of different Protestant traditions. The Civil War had mobilized all American women into benevolent activity on behalf of soldiers and created energy that extended beyond the war. The death of the largest number of men in American history created an entire generation of single women—women who had benefited from the antebellum women's educational movement but who were now doomed to spinsterhood, a despised fate in nineteenth-century America. Male-run denominational agencies continued to drag their feet on the appointment of single women to the mission field, even as competent women volunteered for mission service. The wives of prominent men drew on their social capital to organize women's societies that provided opportunities for unmarried sisters, daughters, and classmates. Missionary wives in the field saw the need to increase the female work force and so threw their support behind the idea of single women missionaries. The result of women working together was a revolution in American missionary personnel and philosophy. By 1890, the infusion of single women meant that women constituted sixty percent of the American mission force.

Unique Contributions of Women in Mission

The subordination of women missionaries to male-dominated norms and structures has had important ramifications for mission theory. By and large women have not concentrated on ecclesiology, or theories of the church, in their reflection on mission. Women have rather concerned themselves with the personal and ethical aspects of mission. Put another way, women's mission theory focused either on personal witnessing or on working toward the reign of God. . . .

"Personal work" was women's strength, as women managed households, nurtured children, chatted with neighbors, and taught reading, sewing, and Western household skills in foreign settings. Women were innovators in making personal connections with indigenous people for the sake of sharing the gospel—adopting orphans to teach them about Christianity, initiating house to house friendship evangelism among secluded women in zenanas and harems, living two by two in *pueblos jóvenes* among the people they went to serve.

The ethical aspect of women's mission theory comes into sharp focus in relation to a major commonality among American women in mission: concern for women and children. From attempts to teach girls to read in the early 1800s, to struggles against footbinding, female infanticide, and child marriage in the late nineteenth century, to crusades for women's higher education in the 1920s, women missionaries incorporated the liberation of women from oppressive social, cultural, religious, and economic structures into their mission theories. Mission work for women included helping them to be better mothers by sharing Western standards of hygiene, nutrition, and health in the name of the gospel. The ideal of the "Christian home," where men and women received equal respect and where children received nurture and consistent care, was an important part of American women's missionary theory and practice, both Catholic and Protestant. Said Nannie Gaines, Southern Methodist missionary who spent forty-five years as a teacher in Hiroshima, "No country can rise higher than her women."[6]

During the peak of "Woman's Work for Woman," women missionaries saw the education of women and children not only as resulting in the Christian home, but as the beginning of social reformation as well. Women missionaries believed the creation of a Christian female elite through the mission schools was a step toward changing societies to be more sensitive to the needs of women and children. As "Woman's Work for Woman" gave way to "World Friendship," such global themes as peace and women's preparation for leadership took on large importance in the mission work of ecumenically minded Protestant women. Special work for women and children has been a priority of women's mission theory throughout most of American mission history.

. . . .

For the earliest Protestant missionary women, to serve as a teacher was living out the Great Commission (Matthew 28:19-20)—as the female equivalent of the preacher. As the value of schooling became apparent for breaking down prejudice against Christianity and for attacking non-Christian worldviews, the role of the missionary teacher provided an entry point for single women to become missionaries. The most influential Protestant missionary teachers were by and large unmarried women: Fidelia Fiske of Persia; Eliza Agnew, forty years an American Board teacher in Ceylon; Ann Wilkins, the most effective Methodist missionary in early twentieth-century Liberia; Mary Scranton, founder of Ewha Women's University in Korea; and Isabella Thoburn, founder of the first women's college in Asia, to name a few.

. . . .

The role of healer ranged from the missionary doctor or nursing sister to holiness and Pentecostal women who experienced physical and psychological healing as a form of evangelism. By 1909, ten percent of the total Protestant woman's mission force had become medical missionaries. . . . Women missionary doctors led in the struggles against social customs injurious to women's health and well-being. To cite only one example, physician Nancy Monelle Mansell was so appalled at the mortality rate of child brides in India, that she led a petition drive to the Indian parliament to raise the age of marriage to twelve. Reformed missionary Ida Scudder, founder of a hospital and of Vellore Christian Medical College, was drawn into medical work by the childbirth deaths of Hindu and Muslim women who had no access to male doctors because of gender-based cultural taboos.[7] To heal women's bodies demonstrated to non-Christian societies that women were the children of God and deserved respect and care. Jesus as healer was a model for medical mission work, especially in his healing of women. In the words of Dr. Saleni Armstrong-Hopkins, a missionary to India in the 1890s, Jesus was "the great Medical Missionary" who became human in order to help, heal, and save his people.[8]

. . . .

The mission theory of American women remained hidden from view because by and large they shared the theological, social, and political contexts of their husbands and male coworkers, yet as lay persons they did not produce the theological and sermonic literature that has set the parameters of discussion. Even in the late nineteenth century, after women had begun to produce mission literature for women's periodicals, men read their papers because of the impropriety of women speaking publicly before men. In the 1930s, a Methodist Episcopal Church, South, missionary woman on furlough who preached regularly at her station was not allowed to speak from the pulpit of American churches.[9]

Without consideration of women's missiological contribution in the history of American missions, the historical record has been distorted and partial. To reflect upon the mission theory of women is to glimpse a vision of the church less an institution than a way of life, as a foretaste of the reign of God that embraces Jew and Greek, slave and free, male and female, "all one in Christ Jesus."

Crossing Borders

Glory E. Dharmaraj, Executive Secretary, Justice Education, Women's Division, General Board of Global Ministries, New York, New York

Excerpted from "Women as Border-Crossing Agents: Transforming the Center from the Margins," in *Missiology: An International Review* (January 1998): 55-65.

The nature of missional imperative is border-crossing as it is spelled out in Acts 1:8. Just before his ascension, Jesus tells his disciples: "You will be my witnesses in Jerusalem, in all Judea, and Samaria, and to the ends of the earth." The nature of missional imperative further is to decentralize, de-essentialize, desegregate, and to be in ministry *with* the constantly changing margins. Border-crossing can be geographical as well as metaphorical. It is crossing the comfort and privileged zones of our lives, going beyond the familiar systems of meaning, and bringing about incarnational mission within our minds, which are often needy sites of mission. It is also sharing the good news and privileges with those who are living on the edges of God's household, the margins of today's societies.

God's core story of mission in the Bible exemplifies the act of border-crossing. The family story of God sending Jesus as a missionary to the world, namely, the story of Incarnation is a border-crossing event. The word became flesh and lived, and we have seen his glory (John 1:14). Jesus reminds his disciples of God's promise of sending the Holy Spirit (Acts 1:4-8). The Holy Spirit sends out communities of faith into the world as people of Christian mission. This is an enactment of the story of continued border-crossing.

Margins often have been coopted by the center.... Sometimes women have been complicitous with dominant forces. In short, they have sometimes been *border-closers* instead of being *border-crossers*. There are women, on the other hand, who have crossed borders and gone beyond the privileges of race, class, culture, and so on, in order to be in ministry *with* rather than *to* people. . . .

Because of the shifting and complex web of forces that constitute marginalization, women occupy several margins according to their social locations due to class, race, culture, and other considerations. . . . For example, if to be a female places one in the subordinate position, and to be a middle class European-American could place the same woman in a dominant position, border-crossing in race relations may become a missional challenge. . . .

Border-crossing is when and where privileged zones are crossed for the sake of mission. This Rubicon of mission is still a challenge to most of us living in the West. How many *border-crossings* are effected in mission is as relevant for mission study as are how many *border-closings* still perpetuated. However, the cross itself continues to be a decentering, de-essentializing, and desegregating agent enabling us as border-crossers. In Christ, there is no male and no female (Galatians 3:28).

. . . .

As for the Methodist stream of laywomen's mission, Barbara Heck became the "Mother of American Methodism" in 1765 when she organized the first Methodist congregation in New York City that included a black woman, Bettye.

The nineteenth century saw the emergence of many women's movements in the United States that worked on social justice issues like suffrage, temperance, peace, children's rights, and so on. . . . The feminine nature of this work was comparable to the leaven at work in a lump of dough: slow yet catalytic. Helen Barrett Montgomery used this image when she wrote:

> It seems such slow work, this gathering of children into kindergarten, this friendly contact with little groups of mothers, this teaching of needle-work. . . . It is woman's work, the patient hiding of the leaven in the lump until the whole is leavened. And there is no agency which has such power to hasten the triumph of the kingdom of our Lord as this hidden work committed into the hands of women.[10]

Gender-based mission has in it an inherent tendency for ghettoization if the mission does not address the general structures that perpetuate inequalities in society. One such major undertaking by the Women's Division of the United Methodist Church toward structural change is in the area of racial justice. A special Woman's Division Committee on Racial Practices created in 1947 made a report on The United Nations Universal Declaration of Human Rights on 10 December 1948 with a recommendation to expand the survey of the investigation into the public laws regarding race and color. . . .

In fact, in 1930, Southern Methodist leaders like Louise Young, Estelle Haskins, and Dorothy Tilly helped Jessie Daniel Ames found the Association of Southern Women for the Prevention of Lynching. The membership of the Methodist women in this was said to have been 55 percent.

In May 1942, the first Assembly of the Woman's Society of Christian Service and the Wesleyan Service Guild was scheduled to take place in St. Louis, Missouri. These groups were comprised of the women organized for mission under the union of the three Methodist traditions: the Methodist Episcopal Church, the Methodist Episcopal Church South, and the Methodist Protestant Church. It was the time when not many cities, including St. Louis, had hotels open to all. Housing accommodation was planned to have the whites in the hotel and the blacks in private black homes. Moved by the conviction that "the Christian Church should lead the way in strengthening the working ideal of democracy" in the nation, the Woman's Division, the national policy-making body of the Methodist women, authorized steps to be taken immediately to change the site of the Assembly to another location. The alternate site of the first Assembly in 1942 was Columbus, Ohio, which had one open hotel. About four thousand women attended. By 1946, when the second Assembly was also held in Columbus, Ohio, there were three inclusive hotels there.[11]

In January 1951, an eight-hundred-page book by Pauli Murray (a young black lawyer with the Home Department of the Board of Missions of the Methodist Church) on *States' Laws on Race and Color* was published, and "it was the first compilation of its kind ever prepared in the U.S."[12] Initially intended as a document to investigate whether the Woman's Division related mission institutions practiced segregation due to the law or to the custom of the states, the document had an impact far above the original intention. The survey revealed that segregation was practiced even when no law warranted it.

The first Charter of Racial Policies was adopted by the Woman's Division in 1952, and it focused on racial policies and practices of the Woman's Division and its network auxiliaries. Prior to the Brown v. Board of Education decision on 17 May 1954, the Woman's Division made a statement calling for building a "fellowship and social order without racial barriers" regardless of the pending decision of the Supreme Court. The second Charter on Racial Policies in 1962 broadened the scope of the racial justice commitment. In 1980, on petition from the Women's Division, the General Conference, the highest legislative body of The United Methodist Church, approved the Charter on Racial Justice Policies as the Charter of The United Methodist Church. The singular and plural in Woman's Division and Women's Division are not interchangeable. The latter is an outgrowth of the former. The change was made in 1968.

. . . .

At the end of the twentieth century, women ask, "Are there women's issues?" Should women be a separate category of mission?. . .

According to the 1995 *Human Development Report* by the United Nations Development Program, globally
- Of $16 trillion a year worth of unpaid work, $11 trillion is done by women.
- Of the 1.3 billion people living in absolute poverty, 70 percent are women.
- Of 129 million children who have no access to primary-school education, 83 million—two-thirds—are girls.
- Of the world's 1 billion illiterate adults, two-thirds are women.
- Of the world's government positions, only 10.7 percent of cabinet positions are occupied by women.[13]

The 1996 *Human Development Report* reinforces the unevenness:
- In industrial countries, the wage rate for women continues to be two-thirds that of men.
- In industrial countries, nearly 130,000 women, ages 15-59, report being raped annually.
- Every year, about 1 million children, mostly girls, are forced into prostitution in Asia.
- About 100 million girls in Africa have suffered from genital mutilation.
- About 80 percent of pregnant women in South Asia suffer from anemia, the highest rate in the world.[14]

The list continues in the 1997 *Human Development Report*:
- About 1.3 billion people live on an income of less than $1 a day. Seventy percent of the poor are women.
- About 700 million people, mainly women and children in impoverished rural areas, inhale indoor smoke from burning biomass fuel.
- If the criterion of the United States poverty line of $14.40 a day is applied, the number of poor by income in industrial countries is 80 million.
- In the United States, more than 47 million people do not have health insurance.[15]

Mission still is challenging and transforming structures that perpetuate such an uneven playing field.

Mary's Song

Mary's Magnificat in Luke 1:46-55 magnifies God as a transformer of unequal grounds. The God of Mary's Song has scattered the proud and lifted the lowly. A song of the transforming mission of God comes from a woman who has surrendered herself to the messianic event in history: the birth of the Savior. She will also one day stand before the cross to see her son crucified. Mary's Song is a song about a resurrected world, a transformed world, a new world ordered by the rule of God.

The Pattern of the Christian World Mission

Lesslie Newbigin, before his death in 1998, was a major influence in ecumenical missions for more than fifty years; a minister in the United Reformed Church (UK) and former bishop in the Church of South India

Excerpted from *A Word in Season* (Grand Rapids: Eerdmans, 1994), 7-18. This essay is the transcript of a lecture presented in 1960.

It is not necessary to speak at great length concerning the changes in the situation of missions. I will very briefly speak of three—first, what one might call the reversal of the tides of world power. The missionary movement as we know it today, the modern missionary movement, took its rise and acquired its characteristic pattern and psychology in a period when the tides of political power, of economic and cultural expansion, were flowing out from western Europe and North America into the other parts of the world. . . . The missionary effort of the churches of western Europe and North America was just flowing down the current, down the stream of world power. For vast multitudes in Asia and Africa, the great fact of our time is not the so-called East-West conflict; it is not the conquest of interplanetary space by man. It is the ending of the era of the dominance of the white races. Missions, which have been accustomed to flowing down the current of world power, are now faced with the necessity of learning for the first time to swim against the current.

The second closely related fact is the renaissance of the non-Christian religions. In the great period of missionary expansion, in the past two hundred years, the non-Christian faiths were to a large extent passive in relation to missionary advance. Today these non-Christian faiths have passed over to the offensive. They are mounting an increasingly effective counterattack. . . . They see the age that has ended as an age in which the white races, the so-called Christian countries, had an opportunity for world leadership and threw it away. I think it is difficult for those who have not lived outside of Europe or North America to appreciate the extent to which our Western civilization has discredited itself before the rest of the world. Our frightful wars, our atomic bombs, and our lamentable moral standards are together quite sufficient to convince most of the non-Christian world that any claim we may make for moral leadership in the world can be laughed out of court. . . .

The third new fact is the rise of "younger churches" to positions of maturity and authority. The existence of a great family of churches in all parts of Asia and Africa and the islands of the sea as the fruit of the missionary effort of the past two hundred years is one of the great facts of our time. . . .

If, as we must do, we acknowledge that the "younger church" is simply the body of Christ in the place where it is set, that it is the church of God, the temple of the Holy Spirit, then it is no longer possible to conceive of the missionary task as something directed from a home base here in Europe and carried on from this base over the head of the younger church in the territory beyond. The center of the operation is there, with the church that God has placed there. . . .

At once the question arises: Is the missionary today an asset or a liability for that church? He (sic) may bring with him very valuable gifts. But his foreignness, his imperfect understanding of the language and the culture of the people, and his obvious connection with the former colonial power may make him in many situations a liability. He may fail to detect the aroma of colonialism that still tends to hang about a mission station even in countries where the colonial era has ended in the political sphere.

. . . .

A New Pattern

The first and fundamental thing that needs to be said about the pattern of the Christian missionary enterprise is that we must recover the sense that it is the enterprise of the whole church of God in every land, directed towards the whole world in which it is put. . . . We need to think of it in terms of the great power of John 17:18, 21: "As you have sent me into the world, so I have sent them into the world. (I pray for them) that they may all be one . . . that the world may believe." We need to think of it in terms of the whole argument of the Ephesian letter, as the working of God to break down the middle wall of partition, and to provide the place of reconciliation where all races and peoples are brought together in a single body through the cross (Ephesians 4:15-16).

In other words, the immediate task of the missionary enterprise today can be formulated in the following terms: to recognize and to draw the practical conclusions from the fact

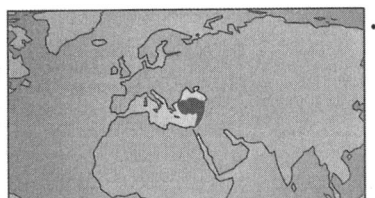
The Church in 100 AD

The Church in 400 AD

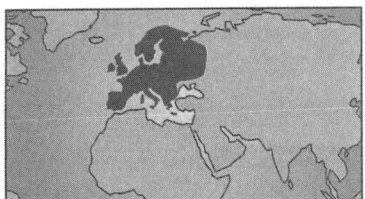
The Church in 1500 AD

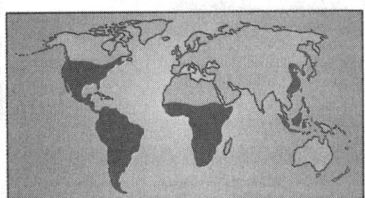
The Church in 1990 AD

- In the first century, the Christian church began as a Jewish church in Jerusalem and then moved to Western Asia, becoming a largely Gentile church with its center still in Jerusalem.

- By 600 AD, the church spread to North Africa and to southern Europe. Its language was largely Greek. The center of gravity of the church lay between Rome and Constantinople.

- By 1000 AD, the church had largely disappeared from North Africa and the Middle East in the face of a surging Islam. The center of gravity of the church now lay in Europe, which was largely Christian by 1500 AD. Theology and mission became largely European.

- By the mid-twentieth century, the church had declined significantly in Europe and the center of gravity now lies in the two-thirds of the World—Latin America, Africa and Asia. Proportionally the Christian church is now non-Western and its theology and mission practice are following suit.

that the home base of missions is now worldwide. The necessity of this task arises from two facts. First, there is the simple fact that the Christian church is no longer confined to a small part of the world, but is to be found in almost every country. The second fact is the rediscovery of the biblical truth that the missionary responsibility belongs to the church as such wherever it is, that the church—as Emil Brunner put it in a much-quoted phrase—"exists by mission as fire exists by burning."

. . . .

This means we must move the Christian missionary enterprise out of the colonial era into a radically new situation. This is easy to say, but difficult to do. . . . What is needed is the widespread and deep recovery throughout the churches, old and young alike, of the truth that to be a Christian is to be part of a universal fellowship in which all are committed to participation in Christ's reconciling work for the whole world. The traditional picture of the missionary enterprise has been of the lonely pioneer going out from the secure citadel of Christendom into the world of heathendom. Today the picture must be redrawn. It must be the picture of one universal family present in almost every land, possessing the secret of reconciliation to God through Jesus Christ and offering that secret to all nations and peoples.

. . . .

The one-way relationship between one body that is always the donor and the other body that is always the recipient does not provide the circumstances in which genuine partnership in freedom can be achieved. . . . The true position of the church is neither dependence nor independence, but interdependence, a mutual interdependence of the different members of the one body that rests upon the absolute dependence of each upon God.

Recruitment of Protestant Missionaries

Joan Delaney, MM, Franciscan Missionaries of Mary, Missionary Resource Center, North Providence, Rhode Island

Excerpted from "A Comparative Study of Christian Mission," U.S. Catholic Mission Association, 1998, pp. 13-14.

In an interview in the newsletter of the All Nations College, a missionary couple lists some of the differences between mission today and mission as it was carried out 40 years ago. Three of the five points refer to changes in the recruitment of missionaries. They note that there is a greater proportion of short-term missionaries and in Protestant churches a stronger emphasis on Volunteer and Youth Programs. Secondly, the article also mentions what the couple refers to as "a change in skin color," by which they mean that missionaries are less likely to be white North Americans or Europeans. Thirdly, in Protestant circles the strong tradition of single women in mission has been replaced by missionary families.

The trend towards more short-term missionaries is also noted in the *Marc Mission Handbook*. This resource lists virtually every Protestant mission organization and denominational mission board in the United States. Recently it changed the way in which it categorized missionaries, classifying them into three main groups depending on the length of service. The categories used are:
- Four years or more—these are considered long-term or "career" missionaries
- Two to four years of service—short-term missionaries
- Less than two years—these can be people serving anywhere from ten days, six weeks, a year, eighteen months or anything in between.

Examining the numbers associated with the categories, the lowest numbers are in the long-term category while much larger numbers are listed for the third category of "less than two years." Given this basic classification based on length of time of service, one is confronted with an astonishing array of recruitment programs in Protestant denominations.

According to the General Board of Global Ministries of The United Methodist Church, there are two main types of long-term service: that of the "career" missionary who serves for three to five years, often renewing the contract, and that of "consultants" who go for slightly shorter periods. The latter are people with expertise either in a secular profession or with skills in congregational development. These two groups combined number approximately 600 people.

A second type of program is for retired missionaries who go back to their previous missions or to another mission for six weeks. The Board is working on including early retirees in a short-term program of this type. These people are not salaried, but may receive some assistance, e.g., housing.

The United Methodist Church has what was described as a "fairly aggressive" program of recruiting local people, particularly from Eastern Europe and the Middle East, to serve in their own local churches. Grants are given to subsidize salaries; training programs are provided by the Mission Resource Center located at Emory University in Atlanta, Georgia.

The fourth category and by far the largest is the Mission Volunteer Program. Not only is this the largest program in the United Methodist Church, it is the largest volunteer program among the mainline Protestant denominations. The program, which is facilitated by the General Board of Global Ministries, is a grassroots organization centered in local churches. There are 40,000 volunteers serving beyond their local communities. They are engaged in construction work, running vacation Bible schools, working with medical and educational teams, as well as being part of faith-sharing groups. In a recent restructuring of the General Board of Global Ministries, home and foreign mission work have been combined, so the 40,000 volunteers may be working in the United States or abroad.

Contextualization in Mission

Donald R. Jacobs, Executive Director, Mennonite Christian Leadership Foundation, Lancaster, Pennsylvania; former missionary in Tanzania and Kenya

Excerpted from *Toward the 21st Century in Christian Mission,* ed. James M. Phillips and Robert E. Coote (Grand Rapids: Eerdmans, 1993), 235-44.

Nairobi, Sunday morning. Contextualization of the gospel in progress! Business-suited parishioners gather at the marvelous cathedral. Up the street comes an animated little string of robed enthusiasts of the African Church of the Holy Spirit, moving to their outdoor place of worship where they beat their drums, worship, and hopefully heal the sick. Within earshot the Legion of Mary, an offshoot of the Roman Catholic Church, is about to say the Mass, in Latin. New forms and expressions of the Christian faith are appearing as regularly, and as predictably, as the harvests.

. . . .

The Gospel and Dynamic Cultures

The gospel enters living, dynamic cultures. The question is: Are human cultures friends or enemies of Christianity? The answer is both. As the recipient of natural revelation no society is bereft of divine grace. . . . Likewise it is evident that all cultures contain some elements that are not at all in harmony with the gospel. It matters little whether one lives in a culture that prides itself on being "Christian" or in a culture newly introduced to Jesus Christ. The gospel is and always will be an intrusion into our cultures; it is an ever new sociological innovation.

Even though cultures are imperfect and often hostile, they are the contexts in which Jesus Christ meets people by grace. Lamin Sanneh reminds us that the gospel moved out of the language spoken by Jesus and his disciples into the arena of Greek. And everywhere that the gospel has been taken since then, enthusiastic evangelists have assumed that any culture can be host to Jesus Christ. A marked difference between Christian and Muslim expansion is that Christians believed the language of the people could fully express and respond to the gospel. Muslims insisted upon retaining the Qur'an in Arabic. In contrast the entire Bible now appears in over 260 languages. As Jesus Christ lived his life within the confines of a cultural context, so can the gospel find a home in any human culture in the world. This might be called the incarnational mode of contextualization.

What is the relationship between the revealed gospel and human cultures? This was the question posed by H. Richard Niebuhr, in his classic *Christ and Culture* (1951). Is Christ *against* culture, *of* it, *above* it, or is he in a *paradoxical relationship to* culture? Does Jesus *transform* culture?. . .

Making the Gospel Authentic in Each New Place

Contextualization is best done by local churches. When missionaries try to do the contextualizing they often miss the mark. In my own missionary career I recall how insistent some of us missionaries were that the local people write their own hymns with local tunes and that they, as a matter of urgency, should employ traditional drumming in their worship services. These seemed to be self-evident improvements. Local hymnody did come—like a storm—but twenty years later, in its time.

Marc Spindler observed, "When Western theologians have given voice to their expectation of an Africanizing or indigenizing of theology, they have met with very marked reserve on the part of the indigenous theologians. Their expectation is considered to be both an incitement to heresy and an insufferable sign of paternalism."[16]

Authentic contextualization is the responsibility of the local believing community. They set the agenda, and they must discern the times. Missionaries at their best should simply be loving encouragers. Often the best contextualizing happens when there is no missionary presence at all such as in China from 1949 until the present.

Von Allmen asserts, "No true 'indigenization or contextualization' can take place because foreigners, the 'missionaries,' suggest it; on the contrary, true indigenization takes place only because the 'indigenous' church has itself become truly missionary, with or without the blessing of the 'missionaries'"[17]

All Christian communities do not do their theology in the same way. In the West, it seems, we do not believe that a theological idea is truly expressed until it is written, footnotes and all, by a qualified theologian. Yet the development of theology in many of the churches of the world, certainly those in East Africa, is done first and foremost through structures: storytelling, art forms, rituals, symbols, and by emphasizing meaningful themes. On a recent trip to the area in Tanzania where I had the privilege of serving as bishop in the 1960s I found that great changes had taken place. In the few days that I was there I heard dozens of songs that I had never heard before. . . . A study of their new hymnody would reveal the directions their theology is taking, as would their preaching and testimonies.

This church is doing its theology, but not by theses nailed to the door or theological tracts as in the days of the Reformation. They are "living" their theology. They are singing it, praying it, preaching it, and expressing it in love to neighbors by praying for the sick and spiritually troubled.

Attributes of a Contextualized Church

I have observed that churches that are honestly seeking to contextualize the gospel embrace four basic assumptions.

1. *A contextualized church is a church in which the basic needs of believers are met in Jesus Christ.* Every culture has many "names" that promise life, prosperity, fulfillment,

security, and hope. Christ-loving believers hear the voice of their Good Shepherd and turn away from all of the other voices (John 10). . . . As social change occurs, new "hopes" appear that often lure Christians to abandon their sole loyalty to Christ in favor of some lesser "name." For that reason contextual theologizing goes on continually in all cultures.

2. *A contextualized church is a witnessing body.* It employs forms, rituals, and behavior that are so relevant and immediate that their unbelieving neighbors receive an authentic and winsome presentation, through word and deed, of who Jesus Christ is. Every generation is responsible to update its expression of faith so that the gospel as lived in daily life does not send a garbled message to unbelievers. The church will so witness to people that whether they receive or reject Christ, they will know precisely who he is.

3. *The believing community will affirm those aspects of the culture which please Jesus Christ.* As noted earlier, all cultures have beautiful aspects that bespeak God's grace. These will be affirmed and encouraged. Christians will incorporate them into their own communal and personal life and will seek to strengthen those aspects in the culture. . . .

4. *The believing community will identify and confront those aspects of culture which are detrimental and not consistent with the gospel of Jesus Christ.* They will not impose their will on the culture, but they will rid themselves of all anti-Christlike aspects of it and will encourage their nonbelieving neighbors to do the same. . . .

Contextualization is never an excuse for accommodating the gospel to culture. Visser 't Hooft observed, "The Christian message has been often uncritically adapted to the national cultures so that its true distinctiveness became lost in the process. . . . In fact there are few of the older Christian nations which have not at one time or another produced curious syncretisms of Christian and national cultural concepts."[18]

If these are the goals of contextualized theologizing, as I believe they are, then all churches and indeed all Christians wherever they are in the world—East, West, North, or South—must seriously ask how their relationship with their culture is consistent with the clear revelation of God in Jesus Christ. . . .

A truly contextualized gospel, by word and deed, will have the same impact today that it had when it was first lived and expressed by the disciples and apostles of Jesus Christ. It is this gospel that turns a city upside down. It is this gospel that heals and comforts. . . . The gospel, authentically lived in any culture today, will have the same effect.

Case Study: Singing the Lord's Song

Thomas H. Graves, President of Baptist Theological Seminary in Richmond, Virginia, *and* **Alan Neely**, Professor Emeritus of Mission and Ecumenism, Princeton Theological Seminary, Princeton, New Jersey

Excerpted from *Christian Mission: A Case Study Approach* by Alan Neely (Maryknoll, N.Y.: Orbis, 1995), 186-90.

Mitchell Hutchison listened with growing dismay and resentment to Richard Farmer's evaluation of the musical innovations Mitchell had introduced in Zimbabwe during the last two years. If there ever has been an example of being "damned by faith praise," thought Mitch, this is it.

Two years earlier Mitchell and his wife Janie had arrived in the East African country with the assignment of teaching in the evangelical seminary and developing a program of musical education and resources for local congregations. Though in his mid-thirties, Mitch had graduated with degrees in Christian education and in music. Furthermore, he had almost nine years of experience working in churches, first in the area of youth and music and subsequently as the minister of music for a large suburban Methodist congregation in Fairfax, Virginia. Those who knew him prior to his missionary appointment described him and Janie as very gifted musicians and effective leaders. Mitch did not consider himself merely a missionary musician, but also a communicator of the gospel and an evangelist.

A Zimbabwe Surprise and New Approach

Extensive readings and courses in missiology had convinced him of the need for contextualizing the gospel not only in spoken word, but also in song. But to his surprise, when he arrived in Zimbabwe, he noted almost immediately how little evidence of awareness there was among the missionaries regarding the "foreignness" of the music in the churches. . . .

Mitch and Janie discussed regularly the multiple evidences of paternalism and the need for change in the missionary approach, and they decided together that their best means of initiating change would be to promote the use of indigenous music in congregational worship. Mitch studied with care the hymnal being used in the churches. It contained, he discovered, almost exclusively European and North American hymn texts and hymn tunes. Even the songs in Shona or Matabele were almost all translations of Western hymns or gospel songs. And in the seminary where Mitch and Janie taught as adjunctive professors, the piano was the only musical instrument used in chapel worship services. Students were not prohibited from using indigenous instruments such as drums, but their use was not included in the musical training program of the seminary.

When Mitch had the responsibility for leading worship for the seminary chapel, he always included the use of the drums, and he insisted on the use of indigenous melodies and texts. He also established three different teaching centers around the country where he went once a month to train local church leaders in worship planning and the use of music in the church. One of his main goals in establishing the centers was the development of persons who would write and promote their own indigenous music.

The general and often enthusiastic acceptance of his work by seminarians, however, was not matched by national pastors and laypersons. Mitch was not prepared for the resistance he encountered in the local churches. Many were clearly attached to what they called "missionary music" that had been introduced by the Europeans and North Americans. Some of the pastors as well as other church leaders told Mitch they regarded the texts as well as the tunes with a high reverence, and they could not envision abandoning their use.

Seven months passed before the first African, a young man from Bulawayo, wrote a song using an African melody and a text reflecting the local setting. The song required a lot of work before it could be presented by a choir, but two months later Mitch taught it to the seminary choir and used it in a chapel service together with three drums and some other African musical instruments. Some of the students told Mitch they liked the song, but no one from the faculty made any comment.

National and Missionary Responses

One afternoon Mitch decided to discuss the matter with Richard Farmer, the newly appointed administrator of the mission. He and his wife Martha had been missionaries in Zimbabwe for more than twenty years. They had stayed when many of the whites had fled the country during the wars of liberation. They had remained when blacks espousing a Marxist ideology gained control of the government, and many of the missionaries asked to be transferred elsewhere. One could not doubt that Richard especially had a deep affection for the people and a strong sense of divine calling to Zimbabwe.

Richard was candid with Mitch about introducing indigenous music and instruments into the churches. He said, "I'm not a colonialist, and I'm not interested in making 'little Americans' out of Christian converts. I am concerned, however, about maintaining the distinctiveness of Christian worship. I find nothing wrong with the use of some indigenous songs, or permitting some forms of African dance, and I certainly don't object to the occasional use of drums in worship. But I am very uncomfortable with the extensive use of drums and especially the use of other indigenous instruments because those instruments and the music they produce are tied inextricably to ancestral veneration. To confuse Christian worship with African traditional ceremonies where beer is brewed and offered to the spirits is a serious mistake, I believe.

"Seventy years ago," Richard continued, "five percent of the country's population was Christian. Today it is sixty percent. Such a rapid change has created a unique set of circumstances. Most people in our churches are less than one generation removed, some of them less than five years removed from paganism. Mitch, we should never forget that. Syncretism of the Christian faith and animism would be disastrous."

Once in visiting a hospitalized child of one of the more prominent national pastors, Richard said he was astounded by what he found in the room. There hanging on the bed above the child's head were several African charms, and the child himself wore two necklaces and amulets that were used by animists to ward off evil spirits. "I knew then," Richard would say, "that most of our people can easily slip back into paganism. How could one of our finest Christian pastors not see the conflict between the old life and the new life in Christ?. . .

"In a culture where traditional ways always threaten to pull people back into paganism, the Christian gospel and the Christian way of life must not be compromised. They must always be shown to be absolutely different."

Growing Unrest and Approaching Conflict

Janie and Mitch, nonetheless, continued to teach part-time in the seminary, and Mitch visited monthly the three centers he had established. Additional indigenous songs were written, and the seminary choir would in the future present them. But a week before the annual mission meeting, Richard called and told Mitch that some of the other missionaries were as concerned as he about the danger of syncretism and the implications of the emphasis Mitch was making on indigenous music. "I plan to raise the issue in my annual report, Mitch, and I hope you will speak to the mission about your work and program."

The first day of the mission meeting included time for Richard to report on his activities and the state of the work. In fact, his report was the last item of the morning session. He concluded with a rather lengthy statement about issues the missionaries faced and a specific reference to the problem of syncretism.

"All of you know," he said, "that this is the second mission meeting that Mitch and Janie Hutchison have attended since arriving in Zimbabwe. We all know that they are a very talented couple, and we are grateful to have them here. Some of you, however, have raised questions about Mitch's emphasis on indigenous music and have asked that we discuss this issue during our meeting. If you approve, we will consider the question of indigenous music as the first item of business this afternoon. I have alerted Mitch to all this and have asked him to speak to us about his work and his plans for the future. I hope we can hear him before entering into any general discussion.

"Do I hear a motion that the suggested order of business be approved?" (The motion passes unanimously.)

By this time Mitch was deep in thought. "How hard should I try to sell them on my program?" he wondered. "Am I the one who is wrong? Or am I simply a 'square peg in a round hole'?"

3. A Shifting Global Context

Introduction

As we explore the meaning of "context," we need to look at the context in our own country as well as on other continents. We must look critically at ourselves, beginning with Kanzo Uchimura's description of our fascination with numbers and technology over spiritual matters (as quoted in Andrew Walls's essay) and Andrew Walls's analysis of the accent on "American" in American missions, to George Hunsberger's statement of how we are satisfied to define church as place, rather than as people or ministry.

The world has entered a new era and Stan Skreslet gives us insight into how these worldviews are changing. One of the most notable shifts impacting Christian mission is the increase in vitality and number of other world religions, particularly Islam. How do we respond to this reality in our own cities and communities?

I once heard Krister Stendahl point out that we always compare our ideal against someone else's actual. That way we always win. If I describe democracy in its most glowing possibilities, and I describe Marxism in its documented shortcomings, which would you choose?

I was once the moderator at an interfaith dialogue. The audience (mostly Christian) criticized the Muslim leader unmercifully for the Muslim role in violence and terrorism. He responded that Muslims "teach peace." One man in particular took exception to this answer and again accused the Islamic leader of teaching violence. Finally, Mr. Naseef answered, "I know that you as Christians teach peace. I also know that Jews were killed in a 'Christian' nation and that 'Christians' dropped the bomb on Nagasaki. Yet I know that you teach peace."

From time to time, unlikely persons hold a mirror before us so that we might see ourselves as others see us. In this moment is a gift that frees us to cross cultural boundaries to witness to the truth Christ offers.

What Is a Context?

Alan Neely, Professor Emeritus of Mission and Ecumenism, Princeton Theological Seminary, Princeton, New Jersey

Excerpted from *Christian Mission: A Case Study Approach* (Maryknoll, N.Y.: Orbis, 1995), 3-4, 8-9.

Though in one sense the Christian faith transcends culture, it can never be communicated nor understood aculturally. In order to be grasped and passed on, it must be transposed from one context to another whether the transposition is the incarnation into first-century Palestine (John 1:1, 10-14), from a Jewish man to a Samaritan woman (John 4:5-42), from a Jewish fisherman to a Roman military officer (Acts 10), or from a Hellenized Jew to Greek philosophers (Acts 17:16-34). . . .

Two conditions appear undeniable and inescapable. First, the gospel is not nor can it be ahistorical. If it is to be understood and appropriated, it will have to be rooted in a particular historical context. But as the gospel is never ahistorical, neither can it be acultural. Christians assert that Jesus was a historical person, and being historical, Jesus was chronologically, geographically, religiously, and culturally a first-century Jew. He neither repudiated his humanity nor his Jewishness.

One can despise one's humanity, but one does not cease being human. One can reject one's culture and discard much of it, but in doing so one never becomes noncultural. One simply sheds aspects of his or her culture and takes up the apparel of another. For every human being or group of human beings is a part of a culture.

. . . .

What then is a context? Max Stackhouse, in an essay written for the Boston Theological Institute, asks the question, "How do we know a context when we see one?". . . Without repeating the intricacies of what Stackhouse says, the following are surely included in those things that determine a context:
- geography
- language
- ethnicity
- political, economic, and social systems
- class, gender, age
- time frame
- sense of identity
- religion
- values
- history

. . . .

Sometimes we assume that our understanding and application of the Christian message is not only an adequate and correct understanding and application, but the *only* understanding and application. Contextualization is an attempt to communicate the gospel in a way that is faithful to its essence, understandable by those to whom it is presented, and relevant to their lives.

The North American Context

Andrew Walls, former missionary to Sierra Leone and Professor Emeritus, Christianity in the Non-Western World, University of Edinburgh, Scotland

Excerpted from "The American Dimension of the Missionary Movement" in *Earthen Vessels: American Evangelicals and Foreign Missions, 1880-1980,* ed. Joel A. Carpenter and Wilbert R. Shenk (Grand Rapids: Eerdmans, 1990), 1-25.

Americans themselves know all too well that their genius is not in religion. . . . Americans are great people; there is no doubt about that. They are great in building cities and railroads, as ancient Babylonians were great in building towers and canals. Americans have a wonderful genius for improving the breeds of horses, cattle, sheep and swine; they raise them in multitudes. . . . Americans too are great inventors. They invented or perfected telegraphs, telephone, talking and hearing machines, automobiles. . . . Americans are great adepts in the art of enjoying life to the utmost. . . . Then they are great in Democracy. The people is their king and emperor; yea, even their God. . . . Needless to say, they are great in money. . . . They first make money before they undertake any serious work. . . . Americans are great in all these things and much else; but *not in Religion,* as they themselves very well know. . . . Americans must *count religion* in order to see or show its value. . . . To them big churches are successful churches. . . . To win the greatest number of converts with the least expense is their constant endeavour. Statistics is their way of showing success or failure in their religion as in their commerce and politics. Numbers, numbers, oh, how they value numbers! . . . Indeed, religion is the last thing average Americans can teach. . . . It is no special fault of Americans to be this-worldly; it is their national characteristic, and they in their self-knowledge ought to serve mankind in other fields than in religion.[1]

The year is 1926; the source, the first volume of the *Japan Christian Intelligencer;* the writer, Kanzo Uchimura, one of the outstanding Christian figures of his day in Japan. He was a first-generation Christian, converted through American missionaries, and full of honour and respect for certain Americans. Of "my own teacher in Christian religion," as he called him, Justus H. Seelye, Uchimura wrote, "I could not but bow myself before such a man. . . . The Lord Jesus Christ shone in his face, beat in his heart."[2] . . . However, for Uchimura, as for a good part of the world, to hear the words *American missions* is to hear first the word *American.* . . .

And to one who had drunk deeply of American missions, it seems that the word *American* conveys, first of all, immense energy, resourcefulness, and inventiveness—a habit of identifying problems and solving them—and, as a result, first-rate technology. In the second place it reflects an intense attachment to a particular theory of government, one that does not grow naturally in most of the world. Third, it stands for an uninhibited approach to money and a corresponding concern with size and scale. . . .

A British commentator can take no comfortable pride in his own position on hearing such an analysis. . . . But insofar as America stands for the West, America is the West writ large, Western characteristics exemplified to the fullest extent. Americans themselves have always been aware that they represent the decisive and ultimate development of the West. None other than Rufus Anderson, an American missionary thinker almost a century before Uchimura, has said:

> The Protestant form of association—free, open, responsible, embracing all classes, both sexes, all ages, the masses of the people—is peculiar to modern times, and almost to our age. . . . Such great and extended associations could not possibly have been worked, they could not have been created, or kept in existence, without the present degree of civil and religious liberty . . . nor could they exist on a sufficiently broad scale, nor act with sufficient energy for the conversion of the world, under despotic governments.[3]

Anderson's analysis refers to the whole Protestant world of his day; but note how easily he passes from the whole Protestant Christian world to a statement that could apply only to the United States. Anderson, however, has no compunction in associating American governmental theory, American continental expansion, and the providential direction of the Holy Spirit.

. . . .

A leading characteristic of historic Christianity is that, though it crosses cultural frontiers, it rapidly acculturates and takes new forms dictated by the culture in which it becomes rooted. It is, then, only to be expected that a specifically North American form of Christianity should arise. . . . Latourette rightly calls the nineteenth century "The Great Century of Missions." But in no part of the world did that century see such a striking outcome as in North America. The main missionary achievement of the nineteenth century was the Christianizing of the United States.

Church: A "place where . . ."

George R. Hunsberger, Professor of Missiology, Western Theological Seminary, Holland, Michigan

Excerpted from "Missional Vocation: Called and Sent to Represent the Reign of God," in *Missional Church: A Vision for the Sending of the Church in North America,* ed. Darrell L. Guder (Grand Rapids: Eerdmans, 1998), 78-87.

Two things have become quite clear to those who care about the church and its mission. On the one hand, the churches of North America have been dislocated from their prior social role of chaplain to the culture and society and have lost their once privileged positions of influence. Religious life in general and the churches in particular have increasingly been relegated to the private spheres of life. Too readily, the churches have accepted this as their proper place. At the same time, the churches have become so accommodated to the American way of life that they are now domesticated, and it is no longer obvious what justifies their existence as particular communities. Discipleship has been absorbed into citizenship.

. . . .

The church may fit well into its social environment, but unwarranted accommodation may cause it to lose touch with its biblical warrant. Or the church may adhere too strictly to scriptural forms of expressing its faith that were intelligible to the cultures of biblical times, and in the process neglect to translate the biblical warrant into an incarnation relevant to the church's current time and place. The struggle to be both faithful and relevant is constant for every church.

. . . .

In lectures in 1991, shortly before his untimely death, mission theologian David Bosch of South Africa put it this way.[4] The churches shaped by the Reformation were left with a view of the church as . . . "a place where certain things happen." The Reformers emphasized that the "marks of the true church" exist wherever the gospel is rightly preached, the sacraments rightly administered, and (they sometimes added) church discipline exercised. . . .

"Church" is conceived in this view as *the place where* a Christianized civilization gathers for worship, and *the place where* the Christian character of the society is cultivated. . . . Popular grammar captures it well: you "go to church" much the same way you might go to a store. You "attend" a church, the way you attend a school or theater. You "belong to a church" as you would a service club with its programs and activities.

Church: A Community of People

In the twentieth century, Bosch went on to say, this self-perception gave way to a new understanding of the church as *a body of people sent on a mission*. Unlike the previous notion of the church as an entity located in a facility or in an institutional organization and its activities, the church is being reconceived as a community, a gathered people, brought together by a common calling and vocation to be a *sent people.* This understanding arose out of global reflections on the church's nature particularly in the light of the worldwide missionary movements of the previous several centuries and the fruit of that work in the existence of new churches throughout the world. . . .

A now global church has recognized that the church of any place bears missional calling and responsibility for its own place as well as for distant places. The church of every place is a mission-sending church, and every church is a mission-receiving place.

. . . .

"Mission" is not something the church does, a part of its total program. No, the church's essence is missional, for the calling and sending action of God forms its identity. Mission is founded on the mission of God in the world, rather than the church's effort to extend itself.

Emerging Trends in Context

Stan Skreslet, Associate Professor of Christian Missions, Union Theological Seminary, Richmond, Virginia, formerly at Evangelical Theological Seminary in Cairo, Egypt

Excerpted from "Emerging Trends in a Shifting Global Context: Mission in a New World Order," *Theology Today* (July 1997): 150-55.

When George Bush offered up the concept of a "new world order" in a 1990 address to the General Assembly of the United Nations, he may have uttered the most enduring and powerful metaphor of his presidency. . . . The phrase abides, I think, because it gives expression to a widespread perception that this is a time of change. As the end of the millennium rapidly approaches, many people—in an astonishing variety of circumstances—do apparently believe that some kind of fundamental shift is underway in their own societies and that complementary forces are at work elsewhere around the globe.

Although one finds broad acceptance of the idea of a new world order, no definite conceptualization has yet taken hold to explain the shape of the new paradigm. In fact, looking back over the last five years, I believe it is possible to identify at least six different ways by which prominent politicians, social scientists, journalists, and commentators have characterized the new world order. These are not mutually exclusive assessments, by any means. In fact, as we shall see, there are certain patterns of interaction that link and interrelate some of these worldviews. They are, however, distinguishable.

A Single Superpower. The vision of the new world order that George Bush proposed in 1990-91 was founded on two essential elements, held in tension. One was the fact that the United States had become the world's sole superpower following the collapse of the Soviet Union. The second was an ideal: the hope that finally the world community of nations would be . . . exercising a greater measure of collective security. What Bush proposed was a unique leadership role for the United States within a loosely conceived framework of increasing global collaboration.

. . . .

Multilateral Global Governance. Crises in Somalia and the former Yugoslavia prompted some to reflect further on the lessons of the Gulf War and to conclude that traditional notions about national sovereignty may soon be replaced by new patterns of global cooperation and governance. According to this view, a commitment to multilateralism is required in the new world order, because some of the world's most pressing problems (such as hunger and mass movements of refugees) resist unilateral or even bilateral solutions.

By 1992, advocates of increased international collaboration began to focus less on the leading role of the United States and more directly on "impartial" agencies—like the United Nations and its extensive administrative apparatus—through which diverse coalitions of states might coordinate joint programs of action. . . . Boutros Boutros–Ghali advocated for the creation of a peace-*making* (as distinct from peace-*keeping*) force that could be dispatched wherever needed in the name of all the world's nations and be managed by the non-partisan office of the Secretary General.

Culture Wars. In the summer of 1993, yet another assessment of the new world order was put forward, this time by Samuel P. Huntington of the Olin Institute for Strategic Studies at Harvard University. His thesis was that "the clash of civilizations will dominate global politics. The fault lines between civilizations will be the battle lines of the future."[5] What drew the most fire in Huntington's article was his assertion that the Iron Curtain of East-West ideological conflict was being supplanted by a cultural clash to be waged largely between the Judeo-Christian West and the Islamic East.

. . . .

Tribalization. This is the idea that the nation-state is becoming less relevant today, because of a widespread process of tribalization that has begun to overwhelm increasing numbers of national governments. Many states are disintegrating from within as the forces of fragmentation, of Balkanization, grow stronger, especially in the weakest nations of the Third World.

A particularly vivid exploration of this phenomenon was offered by Robert D. Kaplan, whose 1994 essay "The Coming Anarchy" appeared in the *Atlantic Monthly*. Kaplan based his conclusions on his own observations made while traveling extensively in the developing world, notably, in West Africa and central Turkey. The new order Kaplan saw being born defies conventional cartography based on the nation-state. Instead, he suggested, the neat lines of national sovereignties are being replaced "by a jagged-glass pattern of city-states, shanty-states, nebulous and anarchic regionalisms" that do not respect or respond to the directives of central governments.[6] When one adds to these a host of countries in which signs of possibly irreparable breakdown are already visible—in Rwanda, the Balkans, Iraq, Somalia, and much of West Africa—it becomes possible to assert, as Kaplan did, that a global pattern of political atomization is underway.

The Century of the NGO. In the 1990s we have witnessed an intense season of global summitry connected with the United Nations. No fewer than seven massive international conferences have been mounted under the UN banner since 1992 to discuss the environment (Rio and Berlin), human rights (Vienna), population and economic development (Cairo), social development (Copenhagen), women's issues (Beijing), and housing (Istanbul). The idea of holding meetings such as these, with delegations sent by member nations, is hardly an innovation. What is new about these gatherings is the addition and growing importance of a parallel conference structure—the Non-Governmental Organization (NGO) Forum—at which the representatives of literally thousands of private volunteeristic organizations meet to discuss the same issues being taken up at the "official" conference.

"The twenty-first century," it has been said, "may very well become the NGO's century—in as much as the nineteenth was that of the nation-state and the twentieth of ideologies and multinational corporations."[7] The degree of change that will be realized in this version of the new world order rests on two factors. One is the ability of NGOs *together* to influence the making of policy whenever delegates of the world's nations gather. But even more important, NGOs *in each country* are expected to assume a role *between conferences*; they are to become the world's conscience, whose task it is to ensure that their governments' promises to the world community are kept and that the obligations of all international treaties and agreements are honored.

The End of Secularism. The 1990s may come to represent, according to this view, that point in modern history at which the relentless march of secularism was finally checked. There is, for instance, the worldwide popularity of Pope John Paul II's books and the very warm reception accorded him even by those who disagree with him on many social issues. Add to this the unabashedly religious vocabulary of the Million Man March and the rise of the Promise Keepers movement. In the 1990s, mainline Protestant denominations are widely perceived as tepid versions of Christianity, while more energetic affirmations of religiosity, like conservative evangelicalism and Pentecostalism, are exploding on all six continents. Another sign of religious resurgence is seen in the growing power of fundamentalist elements

(Christian, Islamic, Jewish, and Hindu) to influence public attitudes and the political process in a wide variety of national contexts.

Some prominent nontheologians have turned recently to religious categories to explain what is different about political discourse in the 1990s. The best-known example may be that of William Fogel, a Nobel laureate in economics at the University of Chicago, who has suggested that America is in the midst of a political realignment, the roots of which are essentially religious. In his 1995 Bradley Lecture, Fogel called this era in American history a "Fourth Great Awakening," an extended period of national religious revival that began in the 1960s.[8] In this vision of the new world order, faith is no longer a private affair; instead, fervent religion is held up as a force that can transform both personal lives and public life.

A Changed Context

Lesslie Newbigin, before his death in 1998, was a major influence in ecumenical missions for more than fifty years; a minister in the United Reformed Church (UK) and former bishop in the Church of South India

Excerpted from *A Word in Season* (Grand Rapids: Eerdmans, 1994), 195-97.

During most of the present century the main global alternative to Christianity has been Marxism. Marxism seemed to offer a practical, this-worldly hope of bringing into being the just society that Christians prayed for but seemed powerless to produce. Marxism was, like capitalism, a product of the European Enlightenment, and it claimed to be able to bring down to earth what Christians looked for in heaven. The claim has proved false, as it was bound to do, but the claim of free-market capitalism to produce a free society is equally false.

I think that in the twenty-first century the main global alternative to Christianity will be Islam. Islam is now, with renewed confidence and with great material resources, making a global claim to offer a kind of society in which God is affirmed as sovereign and all human life, public and personal, is ruled by revealed law. This claim comes into head-on collision with the claim of modernity to provide an open society in which all creeds are tolerated but none except its own is allowed into the public domain. Islam will not accept relegation to the private sector as Christianity has—in many societies—so tamely done. Islam, like Marxism, seeks to identify ultimate truth with actual political power. The union of truth with power lies beyond death, and in that sense Christianity has to be otherworldly. The City of God cannot be built by human hands on earth—it is a gift from heaven. But the Muslim challenge will compel Christians to question the privatization of their faith and to challenge also the idea that public life is an arena from which the truth claims of the gospel are excluded.

I am not here talking about what are called "Christian values." "Values" are merely what some people choose, unless they are based in some reality that is independent of people's personal wishes. When a society begins to talk about values, this is probably a sign of approaching death. Values have no substance unless they are rooted in some reality, something that exists apart from the personal preferences of individuals. I am talking about the truth claims of the Christian gospel, about the affirmations that the church must make about God, human life, and the created world, affirmations that are at present excluded from public doctrine in "modern" societies.

Christian involvement in issues of justice for the poor has been considerably influenced by Marxism. This influence is likely to decrease. There will be a new urgency in clarifying the Christian belief about the possibilities and the limits of human well-being on this side of death, about the relation between God's justification and human justice. Marxism has not been able to deliver what it promised—a human society that overcame the evils of capitalism and created justice and freedom on earth. Capitalism has not delivered such a society. Adam Smith himself was clear that free markets would not work except in the presence of a certain moral framework, and when modern capitalism began to develop in the Western world in the eighteenth and nineteenth centuries, it very quickly become clear that free markets could not ensure a minimum of humane treatment for workers. The market had to be controlled in the interests of human good. The market is the best means available for continuously balancing supply and demand, but it cannot be the ultimate over human life. . . .

We certainly cannot seek the kind of theocratic society that Islam represents. But we can and must affirm that every local eucharistic community where we celebrate the acts through which we are enabled to participate in God's justice and God's mercy is a center from which we can radiate the kind of human behavior in which markets can operate for the common good.

Islam: A Major Factor for the 21st Century

Stan Skreslet, Associate Professor of Christian Missions, Union Theological Seminary, Richmond, Virginia, formerly at Evangelical Theological Seminary in Cairo, Egypt

Excerpted from "Emerging Trends in a Shifting Global Context: Mission in the New World Order," *Theology Today* (July 1997): 158-61.

Islamic fundamentalism is obviously not a new concern for the West, but Westerners' sense of its proximity has certainly been altered in the last few years. Since the World Trade Center bombing in New York, repeated attempts to intimidate Western tourists and expatriates in Algeria and Egypt, and the confrontational postures adopted by some Muslim groups in Europe, extremist Islam has become impossible for Western governments to regard simply as a foreign or remote issue. Moreover, the Western media now routinely describe Islam as one of the fastest growing religions in the West itself. And, as Muslims have become more visible as a faith group in the West, elements within this community have become increasingly assertive about their social and political rights.

. . . .

Islam also cuts tellingly across many liberal theologies of mission. What the razor lays bare is more complex but no less revealing. Many conciliarist leaders, committed to tolerance and interfaith cooperation, are forced by resurgent Islam into a delicate balancing act. Strong disapproval of Muslim extremism is offset by uncritical affirmations of Islam as an honorable religious tradition. . . . Negative comments about Islam are, by and large, reserved for acts of violence perpetrated by religious extremists, who, in the interest of fairness, are usually condemned alongside Christian fundamentalists. No serious attempt is made to grapple with the dogmatic assumptions and assertions of normative Islam. . . .

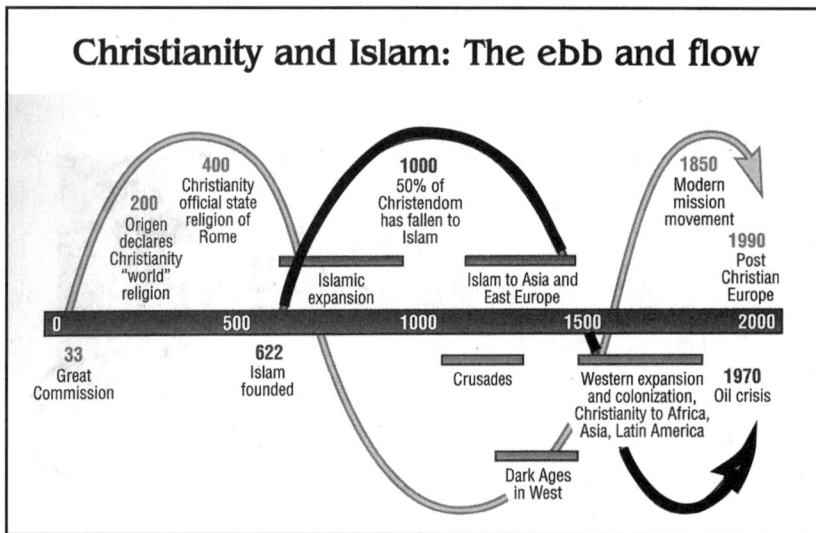

I believe militant Islam is bound to be a debilitating issue for ecumenical Christians in the future. The conciliarist approach to Islam is far too equivocal and nuanced for most parishioners, who would prefer to know from their leaders whether Islam *in toto* is friend or foe. They will get that kind of clarity from conservative evangelicals and others, who will continue to put the case for the direct evangelism of Muslims to a growing and responsive audience.

Obviously, what is needed is another stance, a missiological position that
- empowers Christians to express genuine respect for other religious traditions, including Islam,
- facilitates Christian participation in cooperative civic pursuits, and
- manifests a vulnerable willingness to learn from Muslims and other non-Christian people of faith, but will not tolerate continued indifference to our evangelistic calling.

For Christians, the impulse to share faith and the obligation to love and serve our neighbor ultimately issue together from the same source. It is unnatural and inconsistent when they are unnecessarily separated. The capacity of any theology of mission to hold these twin imperatives together will determine, in part, its adequacy and enduring validity.

Mission and Transformation: A Southeast Asian Perspective

Robert Solomon, Dean of Students, Trinity Theological College, Singapore

Excerpted from "A Southeast Asian Perspective on Mission and Transformation in the Post Cold War Era," in *Mission and Transformation in a Changing World: A Dialogue with Global Mission Colleagues* (New York: General Board of Global Ministries, 1998), 55-61.

The so-called Cold War divided the world into three spheres: the "free" first world, the communist second world, and the largely self-professing nonaligned third world. During the Cold War era, the countries in Southeast Asia (with the exception of Thailand, which had been an independent state), obtained their independence from colonial powers, namely Britain, France, the Netherlands, and the United States.

The Southeast Asian political theater was influenced by three world powers: the United States, the Soviet Union, and China. Generally, the rivalry was between the United States and the other two superpowers. However, there was also rivalry between the Soviet Union and China, although this cooled off as the Soviet influence waned in the region. The question now is whether the Cold War has really ended in Southeast Asia, since communist China is gaining both political and economic influence and the tensions between China and the United States have not ended.

The Waning of the Cold War and the Birth of Hot Economies

When China's Deng Xiaoping rose to power in the late 1970s, China placed more emphasis on economic than on ideological concerns. Deng said that it does not matter whether the cat is black or white as long as it catches mice. This pragmatic drive brought rapid economic growth to China in the 1980s and early 1990s. Now China is aiming to become the world's largest economy in a matter of decades. . . .

The economic opening up of China has not been matched by similar political changes. In fact, this was most evident in what is known as the Tiananmen Square massacre in June 1989. The political leaders of China showed that while they were experimenting with economic liberalization, they were not interested in political liberalization. The Southeast Asian nations tended to side with China, saying that authoritarian governments in Asia are legitimized by traditional Asian values and that the West should not impose its values on Asian nations.

Some Trends in Southeast Asia

We note the following trends in the region:

1. The economy has become the chief concern of many Southeast Asian nations. Anyone promising to help develop the region is openly welcome. Money really talks in this region, as it probably does in other places too.

2. Churches in the region are growing in strength and numbers. Enthusiastic interest in evangelism, vibrant worship, a rapidly growing missionary force, and growing prosperity are all marks of many of the churches in the region. A growing number of young people are enthusiastically committed to the missionary enterprise.

3. With the strengthening of Christianity, we also see a general religious revival in the region. A tightening of ranks, a recovery of religious rituals and rites, and an intellectualizing of the traditional Asian religions are all happening at the same time. Interestingly and paradoxically, there is also a growing secularism fueled by music and media coming from the West. In this melting pot of sociological forces, culture and religion have become more clearly the loci for determining self-identity. A consequence of this has been a growing confidence in Asian cultures and religions. The implications for mission are obvious: a growing need to consider more carefully the relationship between Christianity and culture, and between Christianity and other religions. We must also understand the potential for religious conflict.

Emerging Patterns

Involvement of local churches in mission. When I visited the Lower Myanmar Methodist Church in Yangon two years ago, I met with a cell group from a Singapore church who were there conducting training sessions for church members. In Chiangmai, I visited a small obscure village where a Singapore Methodist church had contributed to the building of a simple hut that serves as a chapel. . . . Mission involvement moves rapidly from financial giving for mission and missionary work to more direct involvement.

Denominational mission agencies. Besides being done at the local church level, mission is also increasingly being done at the denominational level. The Methodist Church in Singapore recently established the Methodist Missions Society (MMS), which has its own full-time director who coordinates its growing involvement in Indochina. In Cambodia, MMS has been able to register the Methodist Church with the government. Two missionaries are already there with a view of setting up an educational/evangelistic mission in Phnom Penh. In the process, a partnership is being developed with other Methodist Churches from the United States, Switzerland, and South Korea. These have been planting local congregations in various parts of the country.

Some Concerns

1. We need to reflect more deeply on the missionary role of the church and the nature of mission. The enthusiasm of the churches in Southeast Asia is obvious and much welcome, but zeal without knowledge is eventually harmful (see Romans 10:2). . . .

2. We need to do mission with great humility. We do not have all the answers and we live in a complex and rapidly changing world. While authoritarian government is still strongly embraced, the economic models of the second world are being discarded. Capitalism, the economic system of the first world, is now encroaching everywhere . . . . . Third world countries have no buffer against the onslaught of a world economic system that threatens the human soul and society. . . . Mission has to be done incarnationally, which means that we must learn to do it with a certain degree of vulnerability and risk, weakness and powerlessness. The cross of Christ symbolizes this very well.

Relating to People of Other Religions

M. Thomas Thangaraj, Associate Professor of World Christianity, Candler School of Theology, Emory University, Atlanta, Georgia

Excerpted from *Relating to People of Other Religions: What Every Christian Needs to Know* (Nashville: Abingdon, 1997), 7-8, 31-35, 101-7.

Ganga and I are fellow pilgrims on the journey of faith. He is a Hindu who teaches Hindu philosophy at a university in Madurai, South India. He also teaches Hinduism to students preparing for Christian ministry at a seminary in the same town. Several times I have gone to the Hindu temple with Ganga. After walking through the outer corridors of the temple and arriving at the inner sanctuary, we would be greeted by a big sign that read, "Only Hindus allowed beyond this point!" This sign was put up recently in response to the insensitive and irreverent behavior of some non-Hindu tourists. Every time we went, Ganga chose not to go into the inner sanctuary lest I feel discriminated against; instead, he would stand at the entrance to the inner sanctuary for a moment, then fall on the floor facing the image of the goddess and pray.

While I stood there next to him lying on the floor, I found myself flooded with questions: Should I also say a prayer silently? Can I pray to the goddess in the sanctuary? Is it even possible to pray to God in this place? If I do pray, will I be compromising my Christian faith? Being Christian, I did not perceive God in the figure of the goddess, because my picture of God has been shaped by the figure of Christ. In that sense, then, I could not pray to God in that setting. But at the same time, Ganga's graciousness in not leaving me alone by going into the sanctuary, the genuineness of his piety and devotion, and his companionship in my faith journey made God's presence very real to me as I stood in that temple. Most often, then, I would close my eyes and say this prayer silently: "God, I thank you for Ganga, a brother in faith, whom you have given me!" That is all I could do.

My visits to the Hindu temple were wrought with dilemmas and questions, but Ganga had a different experience. While he was a visiting scholar at an American university, he attended a nearby Methodist church every Sunday, participating in all the elements of the liturgy, including the Eucharist. When I asked him how he could do this, he told me that he felt as much at home in a Christian church as he would in a Hindu temple. Since there were no Hindu temples nearby, the Methodist church offered him the sacred space he needed to worship God. I marvel at this quite often.

. . . .

Tilaga, Ganga's wife, teaches history in a high school in Madurai. Tilaga is a devout Hindu, yet at the same time she is very open to other religious traditions. During one of our conversations, Tilaga told me about some of her colleagues at school who were Christians. "These are my colleagues, and I love them very much, and they love me as well," Tilaga said. "But every time we discuss religion, these Christian friends will tell me forthrightly, though in a friendly way, that I am going to hell because I am a Hindu, and that the only way I can ever hope to get to heaven would be to believe in Jesus and give up my Hindu religion. . . . What do you say?"

I did not know what to say. I agreed with her that some of my peers in the Christian community did believe that all those who did not publicly acknowledge Jesus the Christ as their Savior and Lord were bound to end up in hell. I told her, as well, that not all Christians believe that people of other religions are damned simply because they are not Christians.

Here is one way of relating to people of other religions: We know and they know not. The basic idea here is this: Christianity is the one and only possessor of the truth about God and the only gateway to human fulfillment and salvation. . . . This view is often supported by quoting the following texts from the Bible:

> I am the way, and the truth, and the life. No one comes to the Father except through me. (John 14:6).

> There is salvation in no one else, for there is no other name under heaven given among mortals by which we must be saved. (Acts 4:12)

. . . .

Instead of allowing these texts to haunt me, I decided to let my experience guide my understanding and interpretation of these texts. . . . But at the same, if one looks at texts such as the following, one gets a different idea:

Then Peter began to speak to them: "I truly understand that God shows no partiality, but in every nation anyone who fears (God) and does what is right is acceptable to (God)." (Acts 10:34-35)

John answered, "Master, we saw someone casting out demons in your name, and we tried to stop him, because he does not follow with us." But Jesus said to him, "Do not stop him; for whoever is not against you is for you." (Luke 9:49-50)

Not everyone needs to be following with us. Whoever is not against us is for us! At the same time, if I use these texts to argue that we do not need to share the story of Christ, that will be equally problematic.

This means that we need to know clearly what kind of document the Bible is. I have found it helpful to say that the Bible is not a book; it is a library. It is a library consisting of sixty-six books. So to ask what the Bible says about our relation to people of other religions in a general way will be the wrong question. No one goes to a library and asks, "What does this library say about other religions?" . . . We need to look at each author, each book, and each subsection to see what we have there. . . . I invite you to closely look at John 14:6 . . . . We may come up with four possible interpretations.

1. Some say that since John's Gospel is more a sermon on Jesus than a verbatim account of what Jesus actually said, one may conclude that Jesus did not actually say that he was the way, the truth, and the life. It is the author, John, who puts those words in the mouth of Jesus.

This interpretation, whether it is right or wrong, is not helpful to me, because whether Jesus said those words or not, John said them, and that matters a great deal to me. Do we not base our beliefs about Jesus, his life, his ministry, and his teachings on the witness of the early apostles?. . .

2. Another interpretation asks the question, What is the situation in which these words were spoken by Jesus? Was Jesus answering the question as to how the disciples should relate to people of other religions? Do we hear the disciples asking that question anywhere in John's Gospel? No, we do not.

Therefore, when Jesus claims that he is the way, the truth, and the life, we see an emerging definition of what it means to be a Christian. A follower of Christ is one who takes Jesus to be his or her way, truth, and life, and one who opts for no other. Such a singular devotion to Christ is what makes people distinctively Christian. To place John 14:6 in today's multireligious setting to judge the destiny of people of other religions would be to take it totally out of its context and derive conclusions that are not intended in that verse. . . .

3. There are some who invite us to understand John 14:6 in the light of John 1:1-18. John begins his Gospel with a poem on *Logos* (Word) precisely because he wants us to view and understand Jesus' life, ministry, death, and resurrection in the light of the portrait of Jesus as the Logos made flesh. This means that the one who is claiming to be the way, the truth, and the life is not simply a man called Jesus in first-century Palestine. It is the Word made flesh who is making this claim. The Logos is in the beginning with God and is God. This Logos is the light of the world, who enlightens every human being (John 1:9). . . . Therefore, in a multireligious context, John 14:6 simply means that God is accessible to all through God's own reaching out to humanity through the Logos.

4. There is another interpretation as well. We all know that the chapter divisions in John's Gospel are not John's own. John wrote the Gospel as one long and flowing piece. The chapter divisions were added much later. Therefore, we need to ask where the incident that leads to Jesus' proclamation that he is the way, the truth, and the life begins. It is very clear that the talk about "the way" begins when Peter asks, "Lord, where are you going?" Let us look at the verses that follow: "Jesus answered, 'Where I am going, you cannot follow me now; but you will follow afterward.' Peter said to him, "Lord, why can I not follow you now? I will lay down my life for you'" (John 13:36-37). By saying, "I will lay down my life for you," he has indicated that the way Jesus is talking about is the way of willing self-sacrifice and suffering. Therefore, when Jesus tells his disciples, "I am the way, and the truth, and the life," he is actually referring to this way of self-sacrifice and suffering.

There is no other way to God, there is no other truth, and there is nothing more life-giving than self-sacrifice and suffering for the sake of others. Did Jesus not go on to say, "No one has greater love than this, to lay down one's life for one's friends" (John 15:13)? Did he not also say, "Those who love their life lose it, and those who hate their life in this world will keep it for eternal life. Whoever serves me must follow me" (John 12:25-26a)? Jesus in this passage is not telling us about Christians' relations to people of other religions; rather, he is

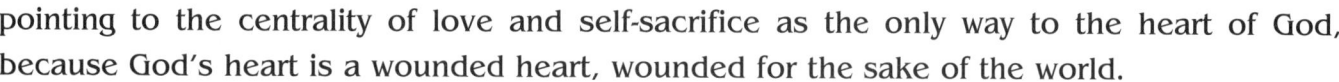

pointing to the centrality of love and self-sacrifice as the only way to the heart of God, because God's heart is a wounded heart, wounded for the sake of the world.

. . . .

It is becoming increasingly clear to me that we need to fine tune our hearts in order to gently and reverently recognize the Spirit of God in Christ at work in the world and among the people of other religions.

Case Study: "What's the Matter, Abdaraman?"

Alan Neely, Professor Emeritus of Mission and Ecumenism, Princeton Theological Seminary, Princeton, New Jersey

Excerpted from *Christian Mission: A Case Study Approach* by Alan Neely (Maryknoll, N.Y.: Orbis, 1995), 78-81. This case study was adapted from Carlo Carretto's book *Letters from the Desert* (Maryknoll, N.Y.: Orbis, 1972).

Darkness was approaching as Brother Carlo emerged from his cell to walk the two hundred yards to the hermitage for evening prayers. His eyes adjusted quickly to the twilight, and, as he expected, he saw his little friend Abdaraman waiting for him. Abdaraman, an eight-year-old Muslim lad, often walked with Carlo, and when invited he shared tea and cakes with the monk. Abdaraman, however, never entered the hermitage; when they were ten or fifteen steps away, the boy would always pull back as if he feared some mysterious force inside would do him harm.

This particular evening, Abdaraman was pensive, melancholy, and unusually quiet. He took Carlo's hand but said nothing.

"What's the matter, Abdaraman?" There was no answer. "Perhaps his father has punished him," Carlo thought. "He will respond because we do not keep secrets from each other."

From Politics to the Desert

Carlo at the time had been in the desert five years living as a monk in contemplation and prayer—a striking contrast to his earlier life. Born in Alessandria, Italy, Carlo Carretto received his degree in philosophy, and while in the university he became deeply involved in Catholic Action, an international anticommunist religio-political movement which began in Europe prior to World War II. From 1946 to 1952 Carretto was president of Catholic Action in Italy. Then at the height of his career he responded to what he described as "the most serious call of my life," the call to separation from the world. Thus at forty-four years of age, Carlo said "yes" to the inner voice that commanded him, "Leave everything and come with me to the desert. It is not your acts and deeds that I want. I want your prayers, your love."

Carretto left Italy for Algeria where he soon joined the Little Brothers of Jesus, a Roman Catholic order of hermits begun to carry on the work of Charles de Foucauld. At the time Carlo had never heard of Foucauld nor did he know anything of the history and rules of the Little Brothers. He only knew that he was entering a community established as a silent witness among the Muslims deep in the mountains of the North African Sahara.

Charles de Foucauld was educated to be a military officer, abandoned his faith, and lived a dissolute life for a time before committing himself to God and the church. He wrote that he heard Jesus saying to him, "Your vocation is to shout the gospel from the rooftops, not in words, but with your life." After a time with the Trappists, Foucauld became a hermit in Tamanrasset, Algeria, in an attempt to reach Muslims by a life of sacrifice and love. No one joined him in his effort, and he did not live to attract a single disciple. It was not until after his death in 1916 and the publication of his personal papers that the order of the Little Brothers of Jesus was founded in 1933, and the Little Sisters of Jesus in 1936, to continue his work.

In many respects, Carlo Carretto's change in life patterned that of Foucauld. Ivan Illich, who knew Carretto as a political leader in Italy, met him again years later in Algeria. Illich, known for his activist community in Cuernavaca, Mexico, said of the meeting, "I came to know Carlo: the man who was dying to the world of power, the world of good causes, the world of big words, and the world of political parties. I came to experience the naked simplicity in the statement of his love for the Lord. I came to marvel at his lack of embarrassment at being judged escapist because he refused to be militant."

Encounter with Submission

Like the other Little Brothers, Carlo lived in a cave near Tamanrasset, high in the mountains of Ahaggar. Though living in relative solitude, he came to know Abdaraman and his father Aleck, a devoted follower of the Prophet. Carlo was unable to ignore the faithfulness of Aleck to the Muslim traditions of prayer, fasting, and sacrifice. Five times daily he prayed; strictly he observed the month of Ramadan; and annually, in homage to Abraham, Aleck sacrificed a sheep in the presence of his family. His absolute trust in and reverence for the will of Allah were as evident as they were impressive to Carlo. Furthermore, though Aleck was dreadfully poor, he continued to work diligently and refused to steal.

On one occasion a detachment of the French Foreign Legion camped along the bank of a small stream that Aleck had kept clear and from which he channeled water for his meager crop of corn. Yet because of the thoughtlessness of the soldiers, the water was being wasted in their washing vehicles and throwing it on each other in jest. The result was that very little water reached Aleck's corn.

Carlo was irritated by the soldiers' lack of consideration, and he admonished the Muslim farmer, "Aleck, unless you say something, your corn is going to dry up and die. Why don't you go to the Captain and tell him that the stream is yours, that you need the water, and they should either use it sparingly or camp somewhere else?"

"No, Allah is great," Aleck replied. "He will provide for my children." So the legionnaires continued to waste the water, and the corn became stunted and died. Aleck's faith in Allah, nonetheless, remained unshaken.

The Question

As they left the entrance to the cave and walked toward the hermitage, Carlo was puzzled by the apparent sadness of his little friend. Was it the water problem or something else?

"What's the matter, Abdaraman?" There was no response.

"Are you hungry?" The boy always had a ravenous appetite, but tonight he was silent.

"Did your father punish you?" Still no answer.

"Did your little bird die?" The boy remained mute.

"Abdaraman, why don't you answer me? You know I am your friend, and it makes me sad when you will not talk."

Suddenly the child burst into tears, and his whole body shook. The tears ran down his cheeks and onto his naked chest and abdomen. Now Carlo remained silent, waiting for the emotional outburst to subside. Then as they approached the perimeter of the hermitage he asked again, "Why are you crying, Abdaraman?"

"I'm crying . . . I'm crying . . . because you don't become a Muslim! . . . If you don't become a Muslim you'll go to hell like all Christians!"

They stopped outside the little mud structure dedicated to Christian worship, a building constructed by Charles de Foucauld who wanted all people to regard each other as little brothers, but who was killed by Muslim fanatics from the same tribe as Aleck and Abdaraman.

Carlo would leave his little friend in a moment and enter the hermitage for prayer. There in the awe and introspection prompted by the Eucharist he would weep as he reflected on the depth of the sectarianism which prevailed and the stain which had penetrated his own soul. On his knees he would recall a traumatic experience from his own childhood when a man came through his village selling a book he had never seen nor of which he had ever heard—the Bible.

He remembered a woman leaning from a second floor window and screaming, "You rascal! Get out of here. We don't want your books! We don't need your religion!" He recalled another woman—who evidently moments before had purchased a Bible—throwing it at the man who was walking slowly down the middle of the street. Particularly painful was the image of the man putting down the heavy bag he was carrying, bending to retrieve the book, and being struck in the back by a stone thrown by a child. The children, many of them carrying stones and urged by the shouting of the women, followed the man as he quickly left the town. Carlo could almost hear the priest congratulating the townspeople that evening, especially the children, for defending the parish from contamination by a "representative of the devil."

Forty years had passed since that afternoon in May, and now the monk was hearing his own faith challenged, not menacingly by an unknown child with a stone, but by his little friend beset with compassionate anxiety. "If you don't become a Muslim you'll go to hell. . . ."

Abdaraman, whose knowledge of the intricacies of theology was nil and who was possibly bewildered by the contrasting lives of this Christian hermit and the "Christian" legionnaires, was heartbroken because Brother Carlo had not converted to Islam. Carlo was stunned. No one had ever manifested this kind of concern for him, and he struggled for something to say.

4. Missional Challenges for the 21st Century

Globalization, Wealth, and Media

Introduction

In the late 1980s, when we thought nuclear destruction was only minutes away, there were historic summits between Ronald Reagan and Mikhail Gorbachev, representing the USA and the USSR. At the same time those summits were held, Christians from both nations participated in prayer vigils. We prayed for peace. None of us could have foreseen the path of world events over the next ten years. I remain convinced of the power of prayer.

On one of these occasions, a young Russian Orthodox priest asked me, through a translator, if he could ask a personal question. In response to my nod, he asked, "Is it really possible to be a Christian in a capitalist, consumerist culture?" (How often have you heard it asked if it is possible to be a Christian in a communist culture?)

This was a "personal" question in that the priest did not want a textbook response. He wanted to know, on a day-to-day basis, if it were hard to be faithful to a Messiah who poured out his very being for others, while living in a culture that promotes individualism and material and economic gratification. How would you answer this "personal" question?

There are many challenges that a mission mind will set before us today. How do we bring a Christian response in a world distorted by inequalities of wealth and opportunity, and with cultural and racial prejudices? How can we stand against the sacrifice of children to the street life, and the treatment of some of God's own children as "nonpersons?" How can we tend God's creation and use God's own Spirit to change the shape of mountains?

"I lift up my eyes to the hills—from where will my help come?" (Psalm 121:1)
"I came that they might have life, and have it abundantly." (John 10:10)

Challenges in the Context of Globalization

Sara Bhattacharji, Professor of Community Health, Christian Medical College, Vellore, India

Excerpted from "Challenges to Mission in the Context of Globalization," *International Review of Mission* (October 1997): 399-401.

We meet at a special time in world history; at the turning not just of a century but of a millennium. What characterizes our times? Can we discern the "spirit" of our time? It is now, as never before, that of a global village. It is difficult today for any nation to remain isolated, pursuing an independent course without relating to others. . . . Within a single day I can be in Geneva from India. A satellite enables me to speak to my cousins in London, Glasgow, and California. Globalization is a process that makes the world one! Sounds good. But what is the "spirit" (essence) of globalization?

Advances in communication and mass media provide widespread availability of information, and, to the few who can afford the use of them, technological advances promise a better standard of living, better health, and longer life. . . . Technology ensures "better" cars, stereo systems, washing machines, and toys. . . . Technology has advanced rapidly. Some technologies have become an end in themselves rather than one of several means to an end. In India, Star TV brings soap operas like *The Bold and the Beautiful* directly, unrevised, from the USA to the villages of Tamilnadu in India. The reverse does not happen, so there is domination of one culture over another. Medical technology ensures longer lives, new kidneys, livers, hearts, faces, and now the possibility of "eternal" life—a clone! The diversity that God saw at creation as "good" is forced into the mold of conformity and we move towards one dominant world culture. Technology, instead of increasing the options people have, is being used to force all towards a few options. We have become slaves to technology.

There is an increase in material goods and a reliance on money as "savior." People are counted as rich by the number of things they possess. Consumerism stresses the need for these goods as a precondition for personal identity, and the acquisition of goods has become the all-consuming passion in many lives. With increasing possessions has also come the need to protect them, and the final result is the use of force by one person or nation against another. Profit for the producer, and not the need of the people, is the force that drives the market. Mammon has become God.

We talk of free markets and claim that more people have more, but the reality is that fewer people control more of the world's share of power and resources; the gap between the "haves" and the "have nots" is increasing, and the consequences are all around us: polluted skies, toxic dumps, advancing deserts, shrinking forests, shantytowns, broken families, neglected children, lonely people turning to sex, drugs, and alcohol for fulfillment. Truly the garden has been laid to waste, joy has been taken out of life, human beings dehumanized, turned into objects and manipulated for profit. The world is split into the consumers and the consumed.

It is in this context that we are called to mission. I believe that our mission remains the same as that of Jesus, of redemption, so that dehumanized people may once again become what they were created to be: whole and restored to joyful relationship with the creation and the creator, as it was when God saw all that God had made and beheld that it was very good.

Communication and Human Dignity

William Fore, retired Director, Communication Commission, National Council of Churches, USA, and first president of World Association for Christian Communication; retired United Methodist pastor

Excerpted from *Church & Society* (November/December 1997): 37-46.

The process most closely associated with human dignity—indeed, with becoming human—is ironically one the Christian community has largely ignored. Communication begins when the newborn child nuzzles to its mother's breast and begins to discover who is *I* and who is *Other*. It continues as the child grows older and communication reveals the differentiations and identifications that result in personality. It is communication that makes possible the creation and maintenance of culture—the language and unspoken rules and values that shape all humans who grow and develop within it.

While Christians traditionally have given considerable thought to face-to-face communication among the faithful, and perhaps even more to activities designed to "communicate" to those outside the faith, they have accorded scant attention to the task of maintaining free and open communication within their culture.

Growing Media Power

The power of media has grown enormously. Technological breakthroughs in the past decade have made communication incredibly faster, less expensive, and more pervasive. Digital communication is transforming all media into a single medium: now telephones can be computers, computers can receive television, newspapers are available on screen, and telephones, computers, TV, and newspapers can all be sent to anyone anywhere on the globe. The potentials for power and profit are enormous. Communication is the fastest-growing sector in the world economy. Already three of the four largest companies in the world, and thirteen of the largest fifty firms, are media conglomerates.

Consider what can happen now that Time, Inc., which owns *Time, People*, and *Sports Illustrated*, and also several book publishers, a cable and television group that includes 767 cable franchises, and much more, has merged with Warner Communications, which owns TV stations, cable systems, book publishers, and a major Hollywood film studio. A book can be published in hardcover by Little, Brown (a division of Time, Inc.), then be "selected" by the Book-of-the-Month Club (owned by Time, Inc.), be given a rave review in *Time* magazine, then issued in paperback by Warner Books, developed into a motion picture by Warner Bros., turned into a TV series by Warner Television, and have a guaranteed run on hundreds of cable TV channels owned by Time Warner.

If a book can be created and merchandised in a dozen different entertainment media and marketed worldwide by a single monopoly interest, surely ideas can be created and merchandised the same way.

Subverting Public Policy

As the reach and power of the communication giants have grown, they have succeeded in demolishing the old patterns of media regulation, substituting the marketplace for public policymaking. . . . But as Dr. Robert McChesney, a media professor at the University of Wisconsin, points out, the market is a highly flawed regulatory mechanism for four reasons:
- In markets, one's income and wealth determines one's power; thus markets support, not democracy, but a plutocracy of the wealthy.
- Markets do not "give the people what they want" so much as they "give the people what they want within the range of what is most profitable to produce and/or in the political interests of the producers."
- Since markets are driven by the need to generate profit, they are utterly incapable of factoring in values that cannot be translated into the bottom line of profits; issues such as universal education, proper health care, full employment, and environmental quality simply cannot be adequately addressed through the market.
- Markets encourage a selfishness that undermines community.

. . . .

A market-driven communication system simply is not designed to do the things that democratic politics is designed to do. According to Benjamin Barber, professor of political science at Rutgers University, commercial television supports only private rather than public modes of discourse. TV allows us as consumers to "speak," but only through our decisions to buy goods. It does not allow us as citizens to talk to one another about such things as the social consequences of our market system, or ask such questions as "Is our nation too materialist?" or "Is there too little justice?" or "Are there too few jobs?"

Christian Strategies

A number of strategies are open to Christians who see this issue as central to human dignity, and therefore to their own outreach as believers.

The first step requires putting to rest the notion that Christians do not engage in social action. Creating changes in the cultural environment to enhance justice and human dignity requires influencing public opinion and getting laws passed.

Second, there is no way that individuals acting alone can modify the imbalance of communication power. Christians must bring to the social scene their moral force in both the local and national arenas.

Third, Christians will have to join with the many others who do not benefit from the existing system. Some of these coalitions will not be easy, since all do not share precisely the same assumptions. Nevertheless, Paul Tillich's concept of the "latent church" must be taken seriously: there are many in the secular world through whom God works with great effect.

Fourth, the church must associate more closely with those who work within the media, some of whom are, of course, Christians. Journalists, writers, directors, and actors are also parents and citizens, and they care about the world into which their children are being raised. . . .

Fifth, the church should support many kinds of alternatives to monopolistic media. This means backing a strong public broadcasting service, one with adequate public funding.

. . . .

Clearly we are all the children of our culture, influenced by it every day of our lives. But Christians also understand themselves to be children of God, and thus to have an agenda different from the agenda of their culture. They aim to let God's light shine into the lives of people, to let them know the saving grace that Jesus represents, to communicate the Good News. They are committed to opening communication at every level—personal, group and, especially today, through the mass media.

Globalization and Communitarianism

Jan Love, Department of Government and International Studies, University of South Carolina, and a United Methodist laywoman

Excerpted from "Contending Forces in the Global Arena," in *Mission and Transformation in a Changing World* (New York: General Board of Global Ministries, 1998), 15-24.

In recent years, journalists and scholars alike have frequently invoked the term *globalization* when examining changes in the world arena. Often left undefined, the word has a variety of meanings. . . . Quotations from two books that discuss globalization give vivid pictures of these processes.

In Chechnya another family member falls victim to ethnopolitical conflict. The value of the dollar drops sharply as the head of the Federal Reserve System shifts U.S. interest-rate policy, causing skittish currency traders to sell billions of dollars and buy yen and marks. The Irish Republican Army resumes its terrorist attacks in London, hoping to force a settlement of the long-standing dispute over Northern Ireland. University students in Istanbul chat with their friends on cellular phones as they sip *raki* in a local bar. Clad in Levi jeans and Calvin Klein designer shirts, their counterparts in Bangkok rock to the sound of Hootie and the Blowfish.[1]

Iranian zealots keep one ear tuned to the *mullalas* urging holy war and the other cocked to Rupert Murdoch's Star television beaming in *Dynasty, Donahue,* and *The Simpsons* from hovering satellites. Chinese entrepreneurs vie for the attention of party cadres in Beijing and simultaneously pursue KFC franchises in cities like Nanjing, Hangzhou, and Xian where twenty-eight outlets serve over 100,000 customers a day. The Russian Orthodox Church, even as it struggles to renew the ancient faith, has entered a joint venture with California businessmen to bottle and sell natural waters under the rubric Saint Sprints Water Company. Serbian assassins wear Adidas sneakers and listen to Madonna on Walkman headphones as they take aim through their gun scopes at scurrying Sarajevo civilians looking to fill family water cans. Orthodox Hasids and brooding neo-Nazis have both turned to rock music to get their traditional messages out to the new generation, while fundamentalists plot virtual conspiracies on the Internet.[2]

. . . .

Economic globalization occurs in finance, trade, production, and labor. Some terms and phrases that echo similar sentiments are: interdependence, integration, economic liberalism, global village, global pillage, "McWorld" (Benjamin Barber), global economy/local mayhem *(The Economist),* videology, modernization, capitalism, the end of geography, the end of history (Francis Fukuyama), and global homogenization.

Some argue that economic globalization has been in progress for several hundred years, as a succession of Western nations have dominated world trade and finance and then competed for colonies. . . . The spread of cheap, high-powered information technology and the rise of global communications during the 1980s and 1990s also fueled the intensification of global economic processes. Roughly 18,000 multinational corporations became responsible for almost eighty percent of international trade.

. . . .

Whereas economic globalization has increased the availability of consumer products to those who can afford them, simultaneously it has removed from their control fundamental structures and processes of decision making about the well-being of people and communities. So far, governments have not been very willing to help use political processes to reclaim much of that control. Interestingly, however, even as globalization has been intensifying, calls for greater attention to community and local groupings have been increasing, both in this country and abroad.

Communitarianism

Communitarianism signifies commitment to the common good, shared meanings, and public spiritedness. It is also the search for a type of community in which the interests and identities of the members intimately depend on and form that of the whole. Communitarianism recognizes and accepts community as a basic human need. Frustration of this need leads to alienation, addiction, crime, and ineffective families.

Some familiar terms and phrases that echo similar sentiments are: traditionalism, conservatism, tribalism, social capital (Robert Putnam), family values, and clash of civilizations (Samuel Huntington).

....

Communitarian calls should sound very familiar to Christians and all other religious people. Religion often provides (or aspires to provide) some of the glue for community life, and certainly Christians promote values like the common good and public spiritedness. At their best, all religions can play a positive role in the creation of life-affirming communities. Yet the distortion of religious commitment and the twisting of group identity can fuel interethnic rivalry and war among contending nationalities. War and attempts at "ethnic cleansing" in the former Yugoslavia demonstrate the negative potential of communitarianism when the search for communities of justice becomes the search for communities of "just us."

....

Conclusion

Increasingly the interplay of these forces offers ordinary people a choice between extreme individualism (which results from globalization) or tribalization into exclusive groups (which results from communitarianism), both of which are violent and militarized. Space for communities where people can make decisions about the fundamental forces that shape their lives is becoming more scarce. Economically, while workers in industrialized countries are being encouraged to consume more, their economic well-being is becoming more at risk. Subjected to the same messages about consumption, poor people simply remain excluded from meaningful economic or political participation. Ecologically, the earth may not be able to bear the weight of greater consumption.

Globalization and communitarianism, however, bring with them opportunities as well as threats. Social movements and churches have access to much of the same commmunication and transportation technology that makes economic globalization possible and they could put it to use for life-affirming causes. The yearning for communitarianism that is evident everywhere presents wonderful opportunities for religious communities to offer life-sustaining, open, and diverse communities that promote a better world for all.

Church in a Market Economy

George R. Hunsberger, Professor of Missiology, Western Theological Seminary, Holland, Michigan

Excerpted from "Missional Vocation: Called and Sent to Represent the Reign of God," in *Missional Church: A Vision for the Sending of the Church in North America,* ed. Darrell L. Guder (Grand Rapids: Eerdmans, 1998), 84-85.

In *The Churching of America, 1776-1990: Winners and Losers in Our Religious Economy,* Roger Finke and Rodney Stark argue that the choice made early on in the United States not to have an established religion meant that an economic understanding of religious life and practice was inevitable. They contend that "where religious affiliation is a matter of choice, religious organizations must compete for members and . . . the 'invisible hand' of the marketplace is as unforgiving of ineffective religious firms as it is of their commercial counterparts. . . . Religious economies are like commercial economies in that they consist of a market made up of a set of current and potential customers and a set of firms seeking to serve that market." Indeed, they suggest that it is appropriate to use "economic concepts such as markets, firms, market penetration, and segmented markets to analyze the success and failure of religious bodies." In their view, then, the clergy are the church's sales representatives, religious doctrines its products, and evangelization practices its marketing techniques.[3]

But here is the rub. Does this image of church correspond to the cluster of images found for the church in the New Testament? Does it correlate with New Testament speech about the nature and purposes of the church? At the very least, this producer-consumer model separates its notion of church (a religious firm producing and marketing religious products and services) from its members (potential and hopefully committed customers consuming those products and services). Members are ultimately distanced in this model from their own communal calling to be a body of people sent on a mission. The gap between these two notions is great, and it is in the transformation from the one to the other that the present challenge before the churches finds focus.

The world by income

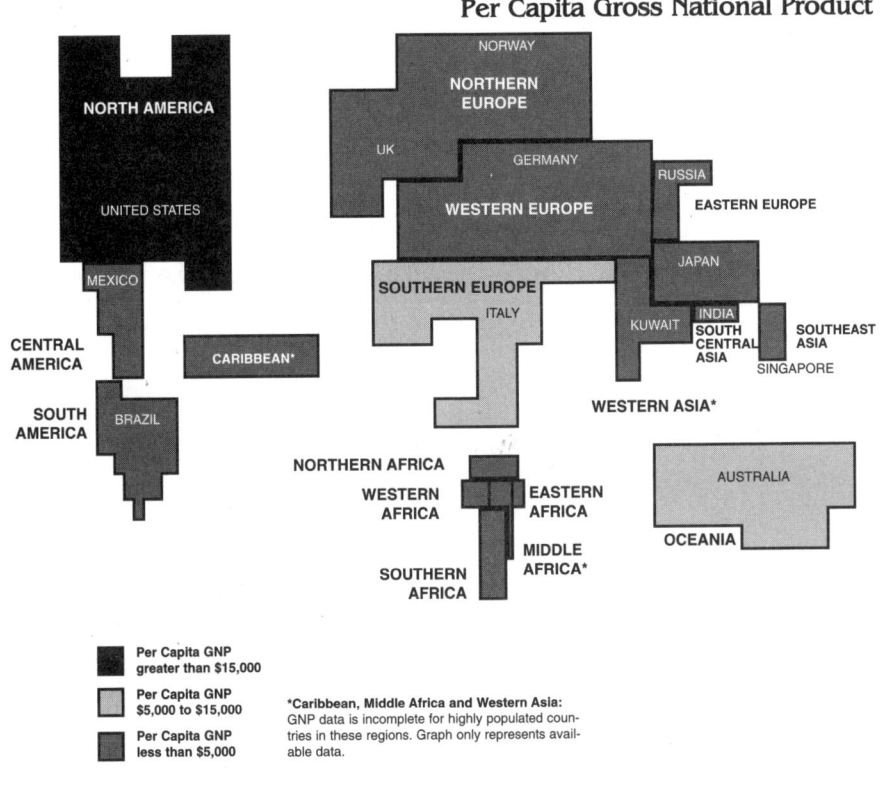

In God's world...
- The northern part of the world dominates the southern part, with North America, Germany and Japan accounting for almost half of the world's income.
- Almost half of the world's families struggle with annual incomes of less than $4,500.
- Of the 925 million absolute poor in the world, 211 million (or 23%) are Christians.

Sources: Barrett, *Our Globe*, 1990; *New State of the World Atlas*, 1995; World Population Data Sheet, 1995

Gross National Product (per person)	
Highest	**Lowest**
Switzerland	Mozambique
Luxembourg	Ethiopia
Japan	Tanzania
Denmark	Sierra Leone
Norway	Nepal
Sweden	Bangladesh
United States	Vietnam
Iceland	Burundi
Germany	Uganda
Kuwait	Rwanda
Austria	Chad

Source: World Population Data Sheet, 1995

Populations, Affluence, and Distribution of Resources

Randolph Nugent, General Secretary, General Board of Global Ministries, New York, New York

Excerpted from his address to the General Board of Global Ministries, The United Methodist Church, October 20, 1997.

Both the greatness and the grace of God beckon us to recognize this particular mission moment at a time when a great mission movement should be, indeed is, possible. All it requires is our placing ourselves as willing partners in our great God's great mission under God's graceful and grace-filled direction.

Our world is fast approaching chaos and collapse. We are living in a world in which understanding, caring, and concern for others have begun to disintegrate. It is a world in which conflicts with weapons are not taking place globally, or even regionally, but a world in which conflicts have become local and prolonged and senseless.

We live in a time in which the quest to accumulate wealth has become so pervasive that the destruction of those who stand in the way of the accumulation of that wealth has become wholesale and the sacrifice of anyone and everyone necessary to the securing of such wealth has become commonplace, casual, and routine. People who labor today without health care–even in the so-called developed nations of the West–is but one sign of wholesale disregard and accepted expendability.

Women, children, and men are abused as overworked and ill-paid sweatshop labor, providing the enormous profits for industrial giants. Today sexual abuse of human beings for profit, sex slavery, and sex exploitation has been dignified with the categorization as an "industry," and takes its place proudly alongside other industrial forms of human endeavor, such as tourism or automobile production.

The world has become so focused upon establishing the worth of human beings only by their monetary value, what they can bring in profit or what they can earn by any means, that the biblical concept of grace has no place in the world's reckoning. Profit and greed have displaced any notion of grace.

Mission Future

New relationships and partnerships need to be explored, expanded, and embraced throughout our global church as we move in mission toward a new millennium. There must be a means to measure mission activity among our mission partners not only as an accounting of how particular grant monies were spent, but also as witness of how the grace of God has touched the lives of mission participants, and how the gospel has been made known and become real and personal in actual human encounters, struggles, searchings, and experiences.

In his new book entitled *Money: Who Has How Much and Why*, political science professor Andrew Hacker from the University of the City of New York concludes with two paragraphs which, although describing the United States could be transposed to other nations of the world.

> How a nation allocates its resources tells us how it wishes to be judged in the ledgers of history and morality. (In this case) America's chosen emphasis has been on offering opportunities to the ambitious, to those with the desire and the drive to surpass. America has more self-made millionaires and more men and women who have attained $100,000 than any other country.
>
> But because of the upward flow of funds, which has accelerated in recent years, less is left for those who lack the opportunities or the temperament to succeed in the competition. The United States now has a greater percentage of

its citizens in prison or on the streets, and more neglected children, than any of the nations with which it is appropriately compared. Severe disparities–excess alongside deprivation–sunder the society and subvert common aims. With the legacy we are now creating, millions of men, women, and children are prevented from being fully American, while others pride themselves on how much they can amass.[4]

The world by population

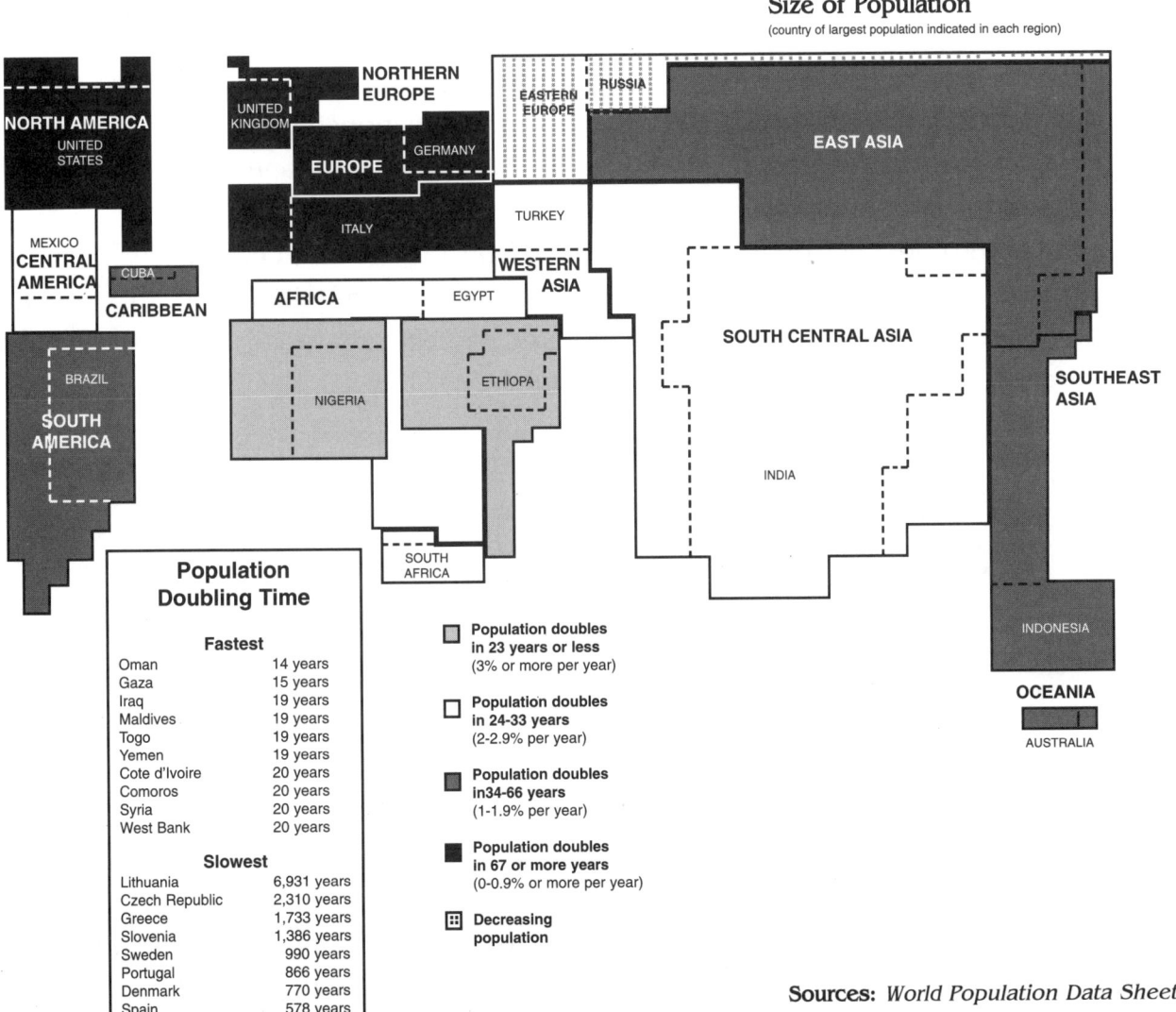

Sources: *World Population Data Sheet,* 1995 and Barrett *AD2000 Global Monitor,* 1993

There is no question that Dr. Hacker's perception and analysis are correct. But there are other ways of perceiving the same reality. Writing in the publication *Hospitality* some time ago, Jim Beaty looked at the same evidence and offered his perception that our confrontation with the homeless is a spiritual litmus test, just as Sodom and Gomorrah were judged not for sexual behavior but for not welcoming strangers. Beaty recalled a bridge dweller who shared blankets with fellow homeless people on a cold night and wondered what would happen if the affluent in our own society were to share in a similar way. As Beaty wrote, there would be plenty to spare if such generosity reigned.

Writing in *The Door* magazine, Bob Lupton offered a somewhat different confessional perception. In watching the poor, he wrote, he saw mothers giving their children's food to neighbors and other relatives. He saw men lending their own rent money for bail to friends who were irresponsible. And he wondered whether such irresponsible acts of compassion would actually mean the poor would be sabotaged by their own hearts and would thus always be poor. He called for a more disciplined approach.

As we move into the mission future, we need both to rejoice and discern in what God is doing in our own doing of mission. And our discernment is clarified and our joy is magnified in company and fellowship with our mission partners. With them we will learn anew of both the person and the activity of God in Christ Jesus.

The Church of the Future: A View from Africa

Mercy Amba Oduyoye, author and theologian from Ghana, Africa, visiting Professor of World Christianity (1994-95) Princeton Theological Seminary, Princeton, New Jersey

Excerpted from "The Church of the Future, Its Mission and Theology: A View from Africa," *Theology Today* (January 1996): 494-505.

The vision I have of the church is quite simply this: It should be a community that demonstrates to Africa how variety and diversity may become a blessing. In other words, it should pick up the traditional African communal principles, enhance them with the good news of Jesus Christ, and enable caring communities to develop and thrive. The future of the church in Africa depends on embarking afresh on its mission to be Christ in Africa. This broad agenda involves attending to several urgent matters, foremost of which are the effects of the global economic system, which, in Africa, manifests itself in terms of national debt and economic structural-adjustment programs that have eroded the sovereignty of African nations and spread militarism on the continent.

Those who watch the world from TV screens can describe vividly what it means to be poor in Africa. The question, Who are the poor? begins to sound like an insult to the thousands whose material deprivations are beyond description. Some of them have heard the Christ preached, and some are even baptized. Others are Muslims, and many hold on to God in other ways. When they are packed together in refugee camps or traveling dusty roads in scorching sun or smoldering swamps in sheets of rainfall, they are humans together. To be church is to have good news for this motley crowd of humanity that pursues fullness of life without attaining it.

The mission of the future church is to respond to all the poverties of humanity, and there is none so poor as the one who does not feel any need. Relatively affluent people living amid persons struggling with abject poverty are often embarrassed to talk about poverty. The poor, on the other hand, are too busy combatting the immediate situation and resisting further exploitation to do any theorizing about it. The church of the future should make people feel the need to talk about justice, peace, and sharing, and not only to talk but also to be challenged to account honestly for their affluence. . . .

When I am confronted with televised scenes of poverty in Africa, I think of the whys and I ask how to stop the carnage. I pray for true wisdom and turn off the TV. But the images do not leave me. Good news is peace, justice, water, and a hug filled with love. But where is the church in all this? My vision of the future church is that it is a community able to be present to the least of the sisters and brothers of Jesus the Christ, . . . to be in solidarity with children, the young people, and the women of Africa, all who are marginalized or fall between the cracks of the planners in church and in government.

A second area of concern for the mission of the future church in Africa is the evolution of culture. The danger posed to the humanity of the African by colonialism, Christian missions, and Islamic resurgence is real. On the other hand, what Africa has to offer to global culture has not been received with honor, and from what I see of the new Christian movements, the only principle from African culture that will be honored and appropriated is the sense of concentric communities that are open. Even this appropriation, however, is not without threat. Community in Africa is being labeled tribalism and ethnocentricity and is being coopted by politicians for divisive and negative uses. The church will embody the good news when it takes into account the dynamism and complexity of African culture and uses its empowering aspects. . . .

When one deals with African culture, specific mention must be made of the role of women. Women constitute the majority in many Christian congregations in Africa. . . . The church's deafening silence in the face of indescribable cruelty to the girl-child as she is prepared to please men is, for me, an indication that the whole church, men and women, has yet to wake up to its total calling. A recent survey of the situation in Africa convinces me that, for most African Christians, most men and some women, it is up to women to demonstrate why the status quo is contrary to the gospel of Jesus Christ. A church in solidarity with women will not only join in eliminating dehumanizing elements in cultural practices both indigenous and imported, but it will also seek justice in the world economy and the end of the use of power for death-dealing purposes. . . . The violence that women endure will be eliminated if the future church will disown all structures and practices that deny the equality of women and men.

It is by doing these and related life-sustaining actions that the world of Africa will come to believe that God sent Jesus Christ to rescue us from the selfishness that leads us to pillage the world and exploit the world's most vulnerable.

. . . .

The future of the church of Jesus Christ is not in human hands, but those who would be part of the future church must intentionally seek to do the will of God in God's world. God wills us good, and Jesus of Nazareth came to proclaim good news to all humanity. The future church will be a community of good news.

Welcoming The Stranger

Who Comes in the Name of the Lord?

Harold J. Recinos, Professor of Theology, Culture, and Urban Ministry, Wesley Theological Seminary, Washington, DC

Excerpted from *Who Comes in the Name of the Lord?* (Nashville: Abingdon, 1997), 19-33, 143-55.

Racism as a Worldview

In North America human differences have largely come to be expressed in the idiom of race. People attribute racial identities to themselves and to others because they believe it is a natural order of things. But the idea of race is not something that objectively exists in the world waiting simply to be confirmed by the empirical sciences. More to the point, race is a cultural category that organizes people's perceptions of one another into racially distinct and exclusive groups.

. . . .

By the fifteenth century, the term race appears in the language of Europeans who ventured into the New World and had contact with diverse cultural groups. In the language of the

French, Portuguese, Spanish, Italian, German, Dutch, and English colonial empires the concept of race is used to classify human beings into discrete and unequal groups.[5]

Racism is a worldview. Essentially, a worldview is a comprehensive way of seeing and interpreting social reality and human interaction in it. The enslavement of Black and Native American humanity served to institutionalize the racial worldview in the Americas. As a worldview, racism conveys that biologically distinct groups are inherently unequal. That the racial worldview whose roots are especially found in the enslavement of Africans was, over time, culturally augmented to include other non-White people is not surprising. Rules of behavior, inequality, exploitation, and social class divisions are assigned by racism.

Race is a symbolic boundary that assures that a social distance is kept between different groups. In North America racism determines residential patterns, quality of education, perceptions of the city and racial/ethnic youth behavior, marriage rules, and church membership. The racial worldview is regularly reflected in cultural forms such as the theater, film, music, art, law, and leisure activities.[6] People simply carry in their heads racist rules for daily interaction with others presumed exclusively different from themselves.

Between the 1950s and 1960s African Americans, Latinos, Asians, and Native Americans mobilized politically to transform the racial worldview of the United States. In the racial movements of the time, both in and outside of the church, people of color found ways to mobilize resources for the sole purpose of eradicating racial oppression and installing a more human social and economic order.

Not Just Black and White

Breaking out of the established biracial understanding of identity in American society also results in a decisive break with the prevailing ideology that turns all Latinos into "unwanted foreigners." In other words, a biracially understood national identity both negates the Latino contribution to national life as well as molds local beliefs that negatively define Latinos as "illegal aliens" or "outsiders" deserving exclusion from the established community.

Surely America's multicultural and racially diverse history on the issue of national identity suggests that no one can unreflectively say Latinos do not belong; yet, Proposition 187 that was passed in California in November 1994 makes such an assertion. Proposition 187 denies public, medical, and educational services to so-called "illegal immigrants". . . It is blamed for the death of Julio Cano, a fifteen-year-old child whose parents were "illegal immigrants" from Mexico. Julio died of heart complications resulting from a bacterial infection brought on by acute leukemia. Julio's parents were denied nonemergency medical services once before in California. With the passage of Proposition 187 they did not take their ill son to the hospital because they feared authorities would report them to the INS, resulting in deportation. . . .[7]

Clearly, Black/White relations in North America will not be the basis for defining national identity into the next century. Quite simply, American society reflects changes that indicate that over the next fifty years 32 percent of the national population will be Latino, Native American, and Asian/Pacific American. Nearly one-third of North American society will be represented by racial/ethnic people of color; furthermore, Latinos will be the majority group of racial/ethnic people of color. . . .

American Christians will draw new insight by thinking of the meaning of national identity in terms that are neither Black nor White. I propose a theology of marginality for mainline Christians to understand the cross of oppression carried by racial/ethnic people. . . . Latinos are speaking of a Jesus who pitches God's tent among them (John 1:14) and calls for the renewal of belief and practices in Christianity.

Toward a Theology of Ministry

In the barrio, Latinos believe too many mainline churches have become mere liturgical centers for hearing Sunday sermons that lack credibility in the world. The gospel's message is not about maintaining inwardly turned mainline churches; rather, it requires churches to discover Christ in the local barrio already renewing people's minds for the creation of a church turned to the world with a message of salvation.

. . . .

As congregations gather for Bible study, worship, and to celebrate the sacraments, they acknowledge the revelation of God-in-Christ. Yet, this visible community needs to be in ministry precisely where the risen Christ is already hidden and waiting to be found: with uninvited guests. Mainline churches will restore meaning to their identity when they recall the gospel's requirement to identify with the barrio. Discovering Jesus in the barrio, hidden in the sick, poor, imprisoned, homeless, hungry, downtrodden, undocumented alien, and underemployed, negates the idea that solidarity with disdained people is optional for Christian ministry. The true church knows it works for justice on behalf of the least of humanity (Matthew 25:31-46; James 1:27).

. . . .

Jesus' story of the great banquet (Luke 14:15-24) is about overcoming barriers to authentic community. Ultimately, Christ, who is the host of the dinner, asks us to overcome our own boundaries of race, ethnicity, gender, class, and culture. The good news of the great banquet is that God loves a party and wills life and approval for all people. God prepares a table of friendship for the uninvited guests in the barrio. Rich and poor. Male and female. Black, White, Brown, Yellow, and Red. All are invited to table.

Amazing Grace

Jonathan Kozol, Boston, Massachusetts, author of award-winning books that examine social issues such as poverty, homelessness, public education: *Death at an Early Age, Rachel and Her Children* and *Savage Inequalities*

Excerpted from *Amazing Grace: The Lives of Children and the Conscience of a Nation* (New York: Crown, 1995), 6-8, 38-39, 123, 129-31, 162, 236-38.

Jonathan Kozol visits the heart of the South Bronx—the poorest congressional district of our nation. He writes about the dreams and feelings of the children there.

Cliffie

A seven-year-old boy named Cliffie, whose mother has come to the church to talk with Reverend Overall, agrees to take me for a walk around the neighborhood. . . . There are children in the poorest, most abandoned places who, despite the miseries and poisons that the world has pumped into their lives, seem, when you first meet them, to be cheerful anyway. Cliffie, as we set out onto St. Ann's Avenue, seems about as buoyant, and as lively, and as charmingly mysterious, as seven-year-olds anywhere. He also seems to feel no shyness and no hesitation about filling the role of guide that he has been assigned.

Reaching up to take my hand the moment that we leave the church, he starts a running commentary almost instantly, interrupting now and then to say hello to men and women on the street.

. . . .

Unlike many children I have met in recent years, he has an absolutely literal religious faith. . . . Speaking of a time his mother sent him to the store "to get a pizza—three slices, one for my mom, one for my dad, and one for me"—he says he saw a homeless man who told him he was hungry. "But he was too cold to move his mouth! He couldn't talk!"

"How did you know that he was hungry if he couldn't talk?"

"He pointed to my pizza."

"What did you do?"

"I gave him some!"

"Were your parents mad at you?"

He looks surprised by this. "Why would they be mad?" he asks. "God told us, 'Share!'"

. . . .

Anabelle

After lunch, I ask the children in a sixth grade class to tell me what they hate or fear the most in life.

Several children answer, "Dying." One boy says, "The rats that have red eyes." A small girl with curly hair and large round plastic glasses says she is most afraid "of growing up." The only white boy in the class and in the school, an immigrant from Russia, says, "What I hate most is the unfairness on this earth."

I ask the children to tell me something they consider beautiful.

Virtually every child answers, "Heaven."

"What," I ask, "is heaven like?"

"A peaceful place with only the innocent," one child says.

. . . .

Later a sparklingly happy little girl from the class named Anabelle sees me opposite the school and walks right up and tells me, "Hi! Do you remember me?"

I ask if I can walk her home, so we can talk a little more. As we walk, I ask her to tell me more about her images of heaven. . . .

"People who are good go up to heaven," she begins. . . . "People who go to heaven wear a nightgown, white, because they're angels. All little children who die when they are young will go to heaven. Dogs and kittens go to animal heaven. But if you loved an animal who died, you can go and visit with each other on the weekend. In heaven you don't pay for things with money. You pay for things you need with smiles."

. . . .

Anabelle's images of heaven give me a delightful feeling that I rarely have in New York City. I speak of these kinds of things as often as I can, and of the feelings children voice for animals they love, because I think they show us something very different from the customary picture we are given of a generation of young thugs and future whores. There is a golden moment here that our society has chosen not to seize. We have not nourished this part of the hearts of children, not in New York, not really anywhere.

. . . .

Anthony

Once when Anthony and I had talked, I had shared with him some of the things that other children in the neighborhood had said in trying to imagine heaven, which he refers to sometimes as "God's kingdom." When I told him what Anabelle had said, he pulled rank of thirteen years of teenage wisdom over Anabelle, who was just eleven, and he said, although politely, that he thought her comments immature. "I think that she's too young to understand."

With the unforgotten habits of a teacher, I had immediately proposed he write a paper for me to correct her misimpressions. (Despite some initial misgivings, Anthony writes the report.)

"God's Kingdom," it begins, much like a homework paper.

God will be there. He'll be happy that we have arrived. People shall come hand-in-hand. It will be bright, not dim and glooming like on earth. All friendly animals will be there, but no mean ones.

As for television, forget it! If you want vision, you can use your eyes to see the people that you love. No one will look at you from the outside. People will see you from the inside. All the people from the street will be there. My uncle will be there and he will be healed. . . . And, as for Edgar Allan Poe, yes, he will be there too, but not like somebody important. He will be a writer teaching students.

No violence will there be in heaven. There will be no guns or drugs or IRS. You won't have to pay taxes. You'll recognize all the children who have died when they were little. Jesus will be good to them and play with them. At night he'll come and visit at your house. . . .

How will you know that you are there? Something will tell you, "This is it! Eureka!" If you still feel lonely in your heart, or bitterness, you'll know that you're not there.

Isabel and Maria

On another afternoon I talk with a group of adolescents who have gathered in another storefront office that is being used as a youth center, this one not in the South Bronx but in a Harlem neighborhood about a dozen blocks west of St. Ann's. When I share with them the statement Jeremiah made about the feeling that he is "locked down," a 15-year-old student, Isabel, jumps right in and says, "I think that that's too strong. I would put it differently."

I ask, "How would you put it?"

"It's not like being in a jail," she says. "It's more like being 'hidden.' It's as if you have been put in a garage where, if they don't have room for something but aren't sure if they should throw it out, they put it there where they don't need to think of it again."

I ask if she believes Americans do not "have room" for her or people like her.

"Think of it this way," says a sixteen-year-old named Maria, who is Isabel's half-sister. "If people in New York woke up one day and learned that we were gone, that we had simply died or left for somewhere else, how would they feel?"

"How do you think they'd feel?" I ask.

"I think they'd be relieved. I think it would lift a burden from their minds."

Conclusion

So long as the most vulnerable people in our population are consigned to places that the rest of us will always shun and flee and view with fear, I am afraid that educational denial, medical and economic devastation, and aesthetic degradation will be virtually inevitable; and this, I am afraid, will be the case no matter what the individual or even shared achievements of small numbers of good human beings who are infused with the essential heroism of the people whom I have described. So long as there are ghetto neighborhoods and ghetto hospitals and ghetto schools, I am convinced there will be ghetto desperation, ghetto violence, and ghetto fear because a ghetto is itself an evil and unnatural construction.

Economic Refugees

Stan Skreslet, Associate Professor of Christian Missions, Union Theological Seminary, Richmond, Virginia, formerly at Evangelical Theological Seminary in Cairo, Egypt

Excerpted from "Emerging Trends in a Shifting Global Context: Mission in the New World Order," *Theology Today* (July 1997): 156-57.

In the 1990s, refugee issues and questions of immigration policy have begun to insinuate themselves as matters of increasing priority on the world's agenda. This is, in part, a result of the fact that the sheer number of refugees clamoring for assistance is accelerating quickly. . . . Sadako Ogata, the United Nations High Commissioner for Refugees, reported to the March 1995 Social Summit in Copenhagen that 9 million refugees had been settled by the UNHCR in the previous five years, but the world's refugee population had nonetheless climbed to 23 million.[8] To 23 million "official" refugees we should add another 25 million persons, internally displaced within their own countries and therefore not covered by the UN's mandate.[9] Then there are those who are not counted at all: the economic migrants who have voluntarily uprooted themselves from familiar but unsustaining rural surroundings in order to crowd into the burgeoning megacities of the Third World.

"Migratory outflows," as this problem is now termed, used to be the result of temporary, geographically isolated conditions of war or natural disaster. What we have now are constant but unpredictable streams of wretched human refuse that not only course through one or two states at a time but are capable of flooding whole regions. . . .

The current political climate in the West is running strongly against the idea of accepting responsibility for economic refugees or even trying to address the root conditions that are producing so many of them. Nearly every leading political figure in the United States—from Pat Buchanan to Bill Clinton—has by now endorsed the idea of imposing more stringent controls on immigration. . . .

My contention is that this situation will eventually evoke a faith response. That is, the crisis of the economic refugee, as a part of the church's context in the new world order of emerging states and now porous Cold War frontiers, will at some point engender renewed theological reflection on the plight of the poor and stimulate new forms of missiological action.

Bridges in Spirituality
Gladys McCue Taylor and Gladys Taylor Cook

Excerpted from *Bridges in Spirituality: First Nations Christian Women Tell Their Stories*, ed. Joyce Carlson and Alf Dumont (Toronto: United Church Publishing House, 1997), 73, 90, 103, 132-133, 140.

Gladys McCue Taylor was born in 1914 in a small house overlooking Buckhorn Lake in Curve Lake First Nation. . . . This community was steeped in the ancient traditions of the Anishinawbe known for many years as Ojibwa. . . . Gladys was a drummer. She was active in pow-wows and sang in the local choir. . . . The Curve Lake First Nation had a celebration day in 1992 to recognize her for being . . . the first Native woman minister.

From a Native Baptismal at Curve Lake Ministry

We sit in a circle as we have always done in any important come together, for the circle signifies the circle of life. From birth until we complete the circle at death the circle of our environment, also the circle of our drum, reminds us all of the heartbeat of every Indian Nation. The four corners of this creation where we are is held up by the four elders, who have their own purpose.

The elder of the North offers the gift of snow and cold air that causes everything to stop their motion, to rest for a season until the elder from the South offers the gifts of warm rain and gentle winds, awakening all that sleep, the trees and herbs, flowers and food.

Then the elder from the East, who is the Keeper of the Light, known to us as the Sun, offers the gift of light and illumination.

Then the elder from the West receives the Sun, who has completed the circle of another day. The other lights, the Moon and the Stars take their place in the sky, telling us of the changing of the seasons and the guiding of our direction. This is the work of the Creator.

Let us always be mindful of this love for us and thank him for who we are. We profess we work for him. Let us try our best to be good leaders and always ask him for directions before we start. For without asking for his help, who are we working for? Will each one who makes up this circle promise the Creator that you will help this child and direct its way to respect all creation and honor the ways of those who have gone before us? So with this eagle feather, we seal our vows, because the feather comes from the messenger who goes closest to the Creator, hearing our prayers from the beginning to the end of our circle. *Meequach* (Thank you).

> *Gladys Taylor Cook was born in August 1929 in a tent, surrounded by fields of ripening rain at Sioux Valley First Nation, in western Manitoba. . . . She was given the Dakota name Topah-hde-win at a special naming ceremony. This name, meaning "four steps," suggests also "help in the four directions," the number four representing the four directions of the sacred circle of life in Dakota tradition. She was later baptized Gladys Evelyn Taylor at St. Luke's Anglican, a mission church in Sioux Valley.*

God's Love

I have always gone to church. After moving to Portage la Prairie, for many years I sat at the back. I somehow didn't feel I was as good as everybody else. It was so hard to believe I had anything to offer. Then one day something happened to make my Jesus become more real for me.

I was at a "Cursillo," a conference to learn about Christianity. One night after we finished our program we were going to communion. I was surrounded by a community of love—and I felt the care and support of the community. As we were going to the communion, they use the word *agape* and said that this special communion on that evening was called *agape*. What they meant by this was *love!* They meant the unconditional love of God.

But the most amazing thing to me was that in my language, *agape* translated literally means bread!

Suddenly I could see that this "love" of God is also the nourishment of my life, my bread. Suddenly I made a deep connection. I felt that God loved me. I felt valuable—just the way I was, just the way I am.

God—God is nourishing. My image of God had changed. I knew always about God. I think I knew about God mostly from Granny Anne. But God was also described at residential school as a God who was watching to make sure you didn't step out of line. The old residential school image of God was negative, a God to be afraid of.

Suddenly, with this agape feast, I knew God to be a God of love and compassion. It was so profound to me. Communion bread meant the body of Christ and the communion connected in the Christian understanding and the Dakota understanding. I felt this overflowing love to be shared, and I had a different personal feeling taking communion then. I think that the people around me must have wondered what was wrong. . . .

Maybe in my heart I always knew about this unconditional love, but this new image, this bread coming together, was a deeper understanding of a God who loves and cares for me.

The next time I went to my church in Portage la Prairie, I marched up to the front of the church instead and sat there. Now I always sit at the front of the church.

. . . .

Our Life Path

We must above all let children know they are spiritual beings and let them know we care for them. Sometimes we're so busy looking after daily chores, we forget to tell them that. We sometimes think they just know that we love them without our saying it. As they grow, we need to respect their choices, even when we may disagree with them. We must always keep the door open to our children and grandchildren.

The drum symbolizes the heartbeat of our mother and offers us comfort and direction all our lives. That's why we have a good feeling when we go to pow-wows. When we hear the drum, it brings us together as part of a big family, and we are all close to our own mothers and mother earth.

God's World, Our Stewardship

EarthCurrents

Howard Snyder, professor and writer, Asbury Theological Seminary, Wilmore, Kentucky

Excerpted from *EarthCurrents: The Struggle for the World's Soul* (Nashville: Abingdon, 1995), 75-77, 177-85, 242-46.

Environment is a word hardly heard when I was young. If used at all, the meaning was psychological: the old debate between heredity and environment in shaping personality. Since the 1960s, *environment* means much more, and *ecology* is now an everyday word. We have witnessed a generational shift in meaning.

Environment means, of course, where we live: our home. Here is the change: We have come to see that the home circle must be drawn larger and larger. Our house is bigger than we thought. It is the whole Earth—maybe even the universe. For all Earth's living creatures, it is especially the terrestrial globe. Earth with its thin skin of soil, water, and air, and the amazing life forms it hosts, is our environment.

This Earth is under siege by creatures who claim to be its wisest, smartest species: Human beings. Technology has now reached the point where it threatens to poison or blow up its own house. Our behavior is suicidal. Leonard Sweet warns: "Thirty-five percent of the oxygen molecules we inhale in one breath comes from the rain forests, which we are chopping down at a rate of twenty-five million hectares a year. Every minute, four football fields of forests disappear from the face of the earth. Every minute, two hundred football fields of arable land disappear under concrete."[10]

Love Your Mother

Economics and ecology form one of the deepest, yet perhaps most hopeful, tensions of emerging global society. Not surprisingly, new or hybrid worldviews start emerging. . . . Enter, then, the Gaia hypothesis, a fascinating and suggestive ecological worldview. Gaia thinking—Earth as a living organism—has become something of a movement. . . . Gaia was the Greek goddess who personified Earth. *Gaia* comes from the Greek word for Earth or land, *ge* (as in our *geography* and *geology*).

The idea of Mother Earth, or Mother Nature as the *anima mundi*, the World Soul, has been a subtheme of Western society since the early Greeks. Always conceived as female, Mother Earth was the source of life on the planet. . . . With the rise of modern science since Galileo and Newton, the idea of Mother Earth became mainly a romantic, poetic convention. Mother Earth disappeared from science. Gaia thinking today, however, is based in cutting-edge contemporary science, especially in ecology and microbiology.

Gaia thinking has been popularized by British atmospheric scientist James Lovelock. . . . Lovelock adopted and adapted the Gaia hypothesis through reflecting on his own study of the environment. He believes that Earth, rather than simply *containing* billions of living organisms, is itself a huge living thing, or at least it acts like one. "I think of the Earth as a living organism," says Lovelock. "The rocks, the air, the oceans, and all life are an inseparable system that functions to keep the planet livable. I now believe that life can exist *only* on a planetary scale."[11]

Lovelock's insights came directly out of his involvement with the U.S. space program. He had helped design experiments to find out whether there might be life on Mars. Looking at Mars, and then looking at Earth as seen from space, Lovelock was struck with the uniqueness of Earth's atmosphere.

> As we move in towards the Earth from space, first we see the atmospheric boundary that encloses Gaia; then the borders of an ecosystem such as the forests; then the skin or bark of living animals and plants; further in are the cell membranes; and finally the nucleus of the cell and its DNA. If life is defined as a self-organizing system characterized by an actively sustained low entropy, then, viewed from outside each of these boundaries, what lies within is alive.[12]

The Ecology of Meaning

The most crucial lesson of ecology, however, is what it teaches about meaning itself. Ecology hints that meaning is found in relationship. A big part of the significance of any one thing is found in its connection to other things. This is another key worldview insight.

At some level, we know this instinctively. We speak of "meaningful relationships," or "significant others." We feel that every individual human life may have meaning. But much of that meaning is found in the relations a person has with other people and with the world around them. People who lack healthy relationships become a menace to society.

Ecology really leads to a deep intuition: *Everything has meaning simply because it connects with everything else.* We may not yet understand the connection or all it means. But if anything is important and everything is linked, then every part is important.

The Meaning of Ecology

The most consistent and credible view of what this means, it seems to me, is belief in a personal God who is both creative Source of the universe and also its Sustainer, Source of direction, and culmination. This is far from being an outmoded outlook. A chief strength of this view is precisely its believability today. . . .

At this point I simply affirm these basics:
- The world is coming to a new ecological awareness.
- We increasingly see that everything is connected to everything else.
- Much of the significance of individual things is found in their linkage to a global ecology.

In the growing global market of worldviews and ideas, the most persuasive worldviews will be those that take ecology seriously.

Earthkeeping

M. L. Daneel, ordained pastor, Dutch Reform Church in South Africa, teaching creation theology and environmental ethics at Boston University, Boston, Massachusetts

Excerpted from *Mission Studies,* vol. XIII-1&2, 25&26 (1996): 130-40.

A growing awareness of the global environmental crisis is manifest in world Christianity. Through the publications of numerous Western theologians our attention is increasingly drawn to eco-theology, environmental ethics, creation theology, and related subjects. . . . Yet, despite these positive signs one cannot deny the fact that on the whole the Christian church as institution has been slow to respond to the environmental crisis in terms of prophetic witness and telling action.

. . . .

In contrast to the global church, African Independent Churches (AICs) have developed in recent years a remarkable prophetic ministry of earthkeeping. There are a number of reasons why a consideration of an AIC earthkeeping ministry in missiological perspective could prove fruitful to the global Christian community. First, the AICs concerned have hardly had any exposure to eco-theological literature and can therefore be said to have developed earthcare concerns in direct response to what they themselves consider nature-related biblical injunctions, relatively free from Western influence. Second, the environmental ministry concerned relates directly to African peasant perceptions and experience of ecological deterioration, such as deforestation, water pollution and droughts, and depleted wildlife resources. Consequently, one obtains an idea of the spontaneous development of a grassroots theology born of existential need in direct relation to local conditions rather than one based on abstract reflection. . . . We therefore need to trace more deliberately the movement of God's Earthkeeping Spirit in today's world if we are to understand the church's mission on this beleaguered planet.

An attempt will be made to briefly sketch the most striking strategy of this movement, combating deforestation through a tree-planting eucharist. . . . AIC theology at best eludes written definition. It finds expression in the throb of celebration; spontaneous proclamation; holistic cleansing of body, spirit, and earth; in rousing song and the rhythm of dancing feet. Its reflection surfaces in communal enactment of richly symbolized ritual and communicates through the medium of stories, told and retold in endless variation. Hence, it is with a degree of trepidation that I, as a white African and "privileged insider," tell the story.

. . . .

A Tree-planting Eucharist

A tree-planting eucharist only takes place once during the rainy season. . . . The pattern of activity for any given tree-planting eucharist is briefly as follows:

Preparation starts with the digging of holes in the vicinity of an AIC headquarters or local congregation. The woodlot is fenced and in some instances referred to as "the Lord's Acre." General ceremonial procedure is in the hands of a principal church leader. A special church committee with future responsibilities such as watering seedlings and general aftercare is appointed.

While the communion table with neatly pressed tablecloth, bread, wine, and a number of tree seedlings on it is being prepared, groups of dancers dance around the bulk of seedlings to be planted, stacked near the communion table. Dance and song bring praise to the creator and great earthkeeper, encourage the green fighters to be vigilant and even implore the young trees to grow well. The service itself comprises several earthkeeping sermons. It invariably also includes speeches by visiting government officials. Thus the outdoor setting, religiously pluriform audience, and speeches of high-ranking environmental and government officials cause the tree-planting eucharist to be an open-ended, inclusive rather than a strictly exclusive, in-group event.

The sacrament itself is introduced by the public confession of ecological sins. All the participants, church leaders included, line up behind a band of prophesying prophets to confess their guilt in earth-destruction. The idea is that the Holy Spirit reveals through the prophets the still unconfessed sins of communicants lest they partake of the bread and wine in an unworthy manner. Thus divine intervention and opposition to wanton exploitation of the earth is vividly enacted.

Each communicant picks up a seedling and moves towards the table as if to draw creation symbolically into the inner circle of communion with Christ, the Redeemer and Lord of all creation. Establishing communion with Christ in this instance is understood as a form of recognition of his role as Earthkeeper and a way of being empowered by him for the earth-healing activity to follow. Meanwhile, one of the AIC bishops blesses the stretch of land to be healed by trees, by sprinkling holy water and scattering holy soil over it. Subsequently, all the tree planters congregate in the new woodlot and "converse" with the seedlings as they plant and water them. In conclusion, many of the tree planters kneel in lines in front of the prophetic healers for the ceremony of laying-on hands and prayer. Thus the healing of the barren earth and of human beings blends into a single sacramental ceremony.

Liturgy Excerpts

A few excerpts of the liturgy (translated from the original in Shona) illustrate essential features of the message conveyed during the ceremony:

Mwari (God) is the one who declares to his church people the value of their friends, the trees—

> They will provide you with shade
> to protect you from the heat of the sun.
> They will give you fruit for you to lead healthy lives.
> These trees will clothe the barren earth,
> protecting it against soil erosion,
> preventing it from turning into a desert,
> keeping the moisture in the soil.

Look at the stagnant water
where all the trees were felled.
Without trees the water holes mourn;
without trees the gullies form,
for the tree-roots to hold the soil . . .
are gone!
. . . .
Let us make an oath today
that we will care for God's creation
so that He will grant us rain.
An oath, not in jest . . .
but with all our heart,
admitting our guilt,
appeasing the aggrieved spirit,
offering our trees in all earnest
to clothe the barren land.
. . . .
Our planting of trees today
is a sign of harmony
between us and creation.
We are reconciled with creation.
through the body and blood of Jesus
which brings peace.
He who came to save
all creation. (Colossians 1:19-20)

Preachers often elaborate on the liturgical text at this point by linking Christ's salvation of all creation to original sin in the Genesis story. . . . Against this background of sin against nature, and God's judgment in response, an urgent appeal is made repeatedly for the confession of environmental sins. Christ is proclaimed as the one who, in the midst of ecological devastation, holds everything together (Colossians 1:17).

The liturgy for the bishop's blessing of the Lord's Acre, where the trees are to be planted, is as follows: The bishop sprinkles the trees with water. . . . "Holy soil" which had been prayed over is then scattered in the woodlot. . . . The bishop leads the green army into the Lord's Acre to do battle against the earth's nakedness; the seedlings are addressed one after the other as they are placed in the soil:

You, tree, my brother . . . my sister
today I plant you in this soil.
I shall give water for your growth.
Have good roots
to keep the soil from eroding.
Have many leaves and branches
so that we can:
- breathe fresh air
- sit in your shade
- and find firewood.

To the Western mind this liturgy may sound simple and only of relative significance, considering the enormous, near impossible task of halting deforestation, desertification, and soil degradation. In the African cultural context, it is, however, a powerful statement of Christian commitment to the healing of all creation.

Healing and Reconciliation

No Nonpersons in God's Family

Donald E. Messer, President, Iliff School of Theology, Denver, Colorado

Excerpted from *A Conspiracy of Goodness: Contemporary Images of Christian Mission* (Nashville: Abingdon, 1992), 91-108.

In today's world the urgency of missional ministry is dramatized especially by the global crisis prompted by the worldwide plague associated with Acquired Immune Deficiency Syndrome (AIDS). We are called to stretch beyond past prejudices and paralyzing fears, creating bridges that will overcome stereotypes and stigmas, bringing Christ's love to all.

Michael Bennett
Dick Hanson
Jerry Smith
Chris Barnaskij
Alfred Gonzales Jr.
Laura Shaeffer

(Director of *A Chorus Line*, a farm activist, a professional football player, a nine-year-old child, a graphic artist, and a physical therapist, respectively.)[13]

. . . .

Albert Schweitzer, noted for his reverence of life, once wrote Norman Cousins about his hospital in an isolated spot in Africa. Schweitzer said, "As you know there are only two automobiles within 75 miles of the hospital. Today the inevitable happened. The cars collided. We have treated the drivers for their superficial injuries. Anyone with a reverence for machines may treat the cars."[14]

John Gaffney
Susan Greenleaf
Stewart McKinney
Margaret Nadawula
"N"
Finis Crutchfield
(A thirteen-month-old baby, an opera singer, a Republican congressman, an African orphan, an anonymous Soviet citizen, and a United Methodist bishop, respectively.)

And the roll call could continue almost indefinitely. More than 126,000 people can be identified by name as having died from AIDS in the United States. Every fourteen and a half minutes someone reports a new AIDS case. Approximately one AIDS death occurs every twelve minutes. One out of every sixty infants born in New York City, most of them incredibly poor, is infected with AIDS. The World Health Organization estimates that by the year 2000 some thirty million adults and ten million children will be infected. . . .

Many of these individuals will be treated by their families, friends, churches, and communities as nonpersons, i.e., persons who do not exist or never should have existed, phantoms to be dreaded and abhorred. No one can predict how many more thousands, perhaps millions, will die from AIDS. Already one out of every ten American families knows someone personally who has died.

. . . .

God's Eye Is on the Sparrow

The conviction that all human life is sacred remains fundamental to Christian theology. . . . Jesus asked, "Are not two sparrows sold for a penny? And not one of them will fall to the ground without your Father's will. But even the hairs on your head are all numbered. Fear not, therefore; you are of more value than many sparrows" (Matthew 10:29-31, RSV)

Artists have often been inspired by the imagery of this passage. The great African American spiritual, "His Eye Is on the Sparrow," has brought hope to millions. An ecological God cares about creation; none lie beyond the pale of God's grace.

I sing because I'm happy,
I sing because I'm free,
For His eye is on the sparrow,
And I know He watches me.

The Hermeneutical Privilege of Nonpersons

Nonpersons are the starting point for a Christian theology of mission. The experience and voice of nonpersons—those who have been marginalized, impoverished, and oppressed—must be accorded a certain "hermeneutical privilege." The missiological accent today, says Christopher Duraisingh, should be on "bringing the peripheral people within the city gate. God brings the marginalized to centre stage, through the work of Jesus Christ, who died outside the gates."[15]

This does not mean that only the poor or the nonperson has a claim on God's truth. However, by first hearing these voices, which historically have been so slighted in mission theology, the possibility persists that we can escape our own cultural cocoons and discern God's liberating and loving initiatives in ways that previously eluded us.

No Nonpersons in God's Family

When William R. Persons formally retired from the pastoral ministry, his wife spoke on his behalf since he had suffered for the previous seven years from Alzheimer's disease and had moved beyond the realm of ordinary discourse. Mildred Persons traced the joys of their earlier ministry and spoke of the grandeur of climbing some of their career summits. But then she recounted the ugly pain of slowly discovering Alzheimer's and what it felt like to become nonpersons.

At that point, however, she paused and in a very poignant moment said:

But, The Iliff School of Theology was the one exception. The Board of Trustees kept Bill as a member. He was sent all the materials. Another Trustee picked him up and took him to every meeting, as long as he could physically attend. After one Trustee session, I asked him what happened. He replied, "I don't know, but Iliff still thinks I'm a people."

Whether it is Alzheimer's or AIDS, whether First World or Third World, whether male or female, whether lay or clergy, whether liberal or conservative, whether urban or rural, whether straight or gay, whether bishop or bartender, no nonpersons populate the inclusive family of God. God's eye *is* on the sparrow!

Forgiveness and Reconciliation

Ngoy Daniel Mulunda-Nyanga, Executive Secretary, Inter-National Affairs, All Africa Conference of Churches, Nairobi, Kenya

Excerpted from *The Reconstruction of Africa: Faith and Freedom for a Conflicted Continent* (Nairobi, Kenya: All Africa Conference of Churches, 1997), 59-84, 126.

Democracy is a source of conflicts. The church as well as policy makers must be aware of the fact that when one talks about democracy, he/she talks about conflicts. Democracy calls for permanent contradictions, negotiations, and agreements. . . .

Another problem is the concept of "opponent" that is at the core of democracy. This concept of opponent raises a cultural challenge in many African settings where the word "opponent" does not exist. In traditional Africa, any person who opposed the ruler was known as "enemy," not "opponent." When one was declared enemy to the king, he was an enemy to the tribe and to all of the members of the kingdom. Such a person had to be excluded from the community.

. . . .

Whenever an opposition leader wants to establish dialogue with the ruling leader, he or she is seen as a traitor and therefore he or she loses the support of the masses.

When one talks about democracy, one talks about coercion, contradictions, debates, disagreements, and compromises. . . . When conflicts related to democracy started to emerge, the churches and other social institutions were not prepared to deal with the issues that were being raised. They were surprised and forced to follow the people's movements; instead of leading and giving an orientation or an alternative to the crisis, the churches became embroiled in the conflicts.

. . . .

Forgiveness and Reconciliation

The management of the issues of ethnicity and nationalism is the major problem facing the African churches in their mission of peacemaking and conflict resolution. These problems are at the center of the debate in Rwanda with its genocide, in South Africa with the Truth and Reconciliation Commission, and in other places at a more local level. These issues become conflicts to be resolved.

The issues of ethnicity and nationalism carry a high degree of emotional excitation and are exceedingly difficult to address. Some people do not want to talk about forgiveness because they think that to forgive is to forget. People who have suffered severe losses prefer justice over forgiveness. These people do not see love and justice within forgiveness. . . .

Many people in South Africa are calling for reparation and restitution. In order to address this issue, the South African government has set up a Truth and Reconciliation Commission whose aim is: "To provide for the investigation and the establishment of as complete as possible a picture of the nature, causes, and extent of gross violations of human rights. . . . This can lead to the amnesty of those who will make full disclose of all the relevant facts. It will also afford victims an opportunity to relate the violation they suffered."

. . . .

The healing of African society will depend on how the churches are going to address these issues. This is the beginning of the church's new ministry in peace building.

. . . .

Church and State: Relations and Conflicts

From the colonial period to the Cold War, the churches in many parts of Africa did not proclaim their autonomy from either the state or the tribal constituency. However, it is easier for the churches to distance themselves from the central state than from the tribes because the tribes are the constituents of many mainline churches in Africa. . . . In the Democratic Republic of Congo (formally Zaire), for example, the Protestant denominations were established according to regions and tribes. . . .

When the states were forced to authorize the creation of many political parties, the parties used the same tribal constituencies. Many tribes were encouraged to form political parties because of the oppression and injustice that they suffered during the dictatorship. For them the call for democracy was an opportunity for equal rights and justice.

In Togo, for example, the Mina, mostly Methodists, felt oppressed since the assassination of the first president in 1963. Since that period, they did not see themselves as part of the governing system. When the opposition parties were formed, it seemed that the Methodist Church became the church of the opposition due to its membership. In Burundi, the Methodists are mostly Hutu and the majority of Tutsi are Anglicans. With the politico-ethnic conflict going on in the country, most of the Hutus are out of the capital city, Bujumbura, while some are refugees in Kenya and Congo. The Anglicans seem to be safe in the country because most of the members are Tutsi who also control the army. However, one cannot simply say whether it is a war between the Anglicans and the Methodists, or a war between the Tutsi and the Hutu. Or is it a war between the Hutu ruling party and the Tutsi army?

. . . .

In this complex situation, what should the church do? Can the church get out of politics in order to be safe? Should the church keep quiet before injustice and oppression? With the reality of tribal and ethnic conflict in Africa, how is the church going to deal with these issues in her ministry without being a target of violence and an element of division in the community?

Politics and the Church

African churches must educate and prepare their members to play active roles in political life. Our churches have spent a lot of time preparing the members to care for heaven; let us mobilize the same people to make sure that they do not tolerate any government that dehumanizes this continent.

The church of the twenty-first century must be the place where issues such as democracy, human rights, constitutional reforms, sexuality, tribalism, and ethnicity must be discussed and analyzed. Any political issue that seems to have direct implications for the lives of the poor and the oppressed must find a place for open discussion in the church. . . .

The churches of the future must be the place where those who are persecuted must feel safe and welcomed. It is sad to admit that African churches have become the most insecure places to hide. The killing of seven hundred Christians in Liberia during the civil war and the slaughter of hundreds of thousands in the genocide in Rwanda are bitter memories and testimonies for the church. The image of the church must be changed. Human rights activists, prodemocracy lobbyists, refugees, illegal immigrants, and opposition leaders must feel safe in the House of the Lord. Pastors and priests are not security agents to disclose the venue where children of God are hiding to save their lives; they have the prime responsibility to save life and to protect whoever is in the temple.

It is my faith that our churches will help Africa to enter the land of freedom, of true democracy, and of peace and justice for all our people. If we do so, we shall be God's faithful servants.

Tending God's Children

Children and Poverty: An Episcopal Initiative

The Council of Bishops of The United Methodist Church believes that God is calling this church to a new level of dedication and commitment on behalf of children and the impoverished. The council is taking steps, through the Episcopal Initiative on Children and Poverty, to assist the church in responding to God's call.

The Crisis among Children

Child sacrifice has been taboo among the world's great religions for at least three thousand years, yet today children are being sacrificed to the gods of consumerism, violence, and neglect. Economic injustice, racial and ethnic and religious hatred, and the abuse of political power are resulting in the genocide of the world's most vulnerable citizens, children who live in poverty.

Malnutrition kills an estimated thirty-five thousand children every day. Approximately ten million children die of poverty-related causes each year. During the last decade alone, wars have slaughtered two million and disabled between four and five million children. More than five million have been forced into refugee camps and at least twelve million have been left without homes. More children than soldiers now die from war. Twelve million of the world's children are growing up homeless.[16] Some eighty million children between the ages of ten and fourteen work for low wages in often dangerous conditions to supply inexpensive products for citizens of more affluent nations.

. . . .

An increasing number of children in the United States suffer from the demons of violence, poverty, neglect, and inadequate health care. The gap between the rich and poor in the United States is wider than at any time since World War II. . . .

The United States now has the highest rate of poverty in more than thirty years. More than fifteen million American children live in poverty, nine million lack basic health care, and preschool vaccinations lag behind those in some Third World nations.

. . . .

Methodism, Children, and the Poor

Methodism was born among the impoverished of eighteenth-century England. Studies document that the poor were the central focus of the early Methodist movement. . . . Wesley considered regular visitation of the poor a necessary spiritual discipline. He would no more neglect regular visitation of the poor than he would miss partaking of the Eucharist. The poor literally accompanied him to his grave. As directed in his last will and testament, he was carried to his grave by six poor people who were paid one pound each. The black drapings used in the chapel for his memorial service were remade into dresses and distributed to poor women.[17]

Children and their total needs were of particular concern to the early Methodists. Wesley was especially concerned that impoverished children not only learn "to read, write, and cast accounts, but more especially (by God's assistance) to 'know God and Jesus Christ whom he hath sent.'"[18] Methodist preachers were expected to spend time with the children. Some preachers hesitated, claiming, "But I have no gift for this." Wesley's firm response was, "Gift or no gift, you are to do it, else you are not called to be a Methodist preacher."[19]

Wesley's commitment to children and the impoverished went beyond friendship and proclamation. He provided education, opened free health clinics, established a sewing cooperative for women in poverty, provided a lending agency, opposed slavery, and visited the imprisoned. Methodism in the eighteenth century was a movement of the poor, by the poor, and for the poor; and Wesley considered affluence the most serious threat to the continued vitality and faithfulness of the Methodist movement.[20]

. . . .

Francis Asbury shared the Wesleyan evangelical zeal for the poor. He warned the preachers that faithfulness requires that they be among the poor. Gradually, however, the church distanced itself from the poor, who became objects of mission rather than constitutive to the life of the church. That trend has continued to this day, and the poor are seldom present in our worship and fellowship. . . .

The American church may be fulfilling Wesley's fear of the consequences of affluence and separation from the impoverished: having the form of religion but lacking its power. A church separated from "the least of these" is separated from the source of its identity and power, the God who is among the most vulnerable.

. . . .

Primary Goal of the Initiative

The primary goal is evangelization, the proclamation in word and deed of the gospel of God's redeeming, reconciling, and transforming grace in Jesus Christ to and with the children and those oppressed by poverty. The United Methodist Church is called to be a means of grace to the vulnerable. The Church must also be open and hospitable to God's transforming grace *through* the vulnerable. . . . It must nurture and build just, hospitable, and compassionate communities in which the least have access to God's table of abundance.

The Shape of Your Mountain

Mary Taylor Previte, born in China of missionary parents, director of Camden County Youth Center, Camden, New Jersey

Excerpted from "You Can Change the Shape of Your Mountain," in *Children and Violence* (Federal Way, Wash.: World Vision, 1995), 25-35.

A young traveler on the mountainside of the Alps was puzzled as he watched in the distance an old shepherd among a herd of puny sheep and goats. The traveler saw the gnarled old hand reach down into a battered bucket draped over his arm and pluck something so tiny out. Then with his shepherd's crook he pierced the mountainside and dropped this tiny thing into the ground and then reached out his foot so softly and packed the ground.

And the traveler called down, "Old shepherd! What is that you are doing here on this Godforsaken mountainside?" And the old man looked up as though it seemed so obvious.

"Why, I am changing the shape of my mountain." The young man drew back and sneered, "No one changes the shape of a mountain."

. . . .

The traveler walked sadly away because he knew in his heart no one changes the shape of a mountain.

Then the traveler himself grew old and dreamed of taking a nostalgic trip. The map in his hands said he'd reached the mountain, but now nothing seemed the same. For where once he had seen a Godforsaken barren hillside, he now saw giant oak trees. He saw little children running down country pathways. He saw villages nestled under massive branches. He heard birds singing overhead. And then he remembered one old shepherd who believed he could change the shape of his mountain.

Come with Me to This Mountain

For these few minutes would you just take one woman's hand who, 20 years ago, stepped out onto America's mountain and believed she could change that mountain. But it's not just Mary's mountain. It's your mountain . . . where every five minutes a child is arrested for a violent crime. Where every five seconds of the school day a child drops out of school. Where every 26 seconds a child runs away from home. Where every four hours a child commits suicide. Where every 36 minutes a child is killed or injured by a gun.

Yet those are faceless numbers, and I want you to see faces. I want you to come on this mountain where Michael too often knows his father's name, but not his face. Where Michelle dreams of being a hairdresser, but grows up to be a whore. Where Angel, a child of 10, can tell me how to train a killer pit bull, but cannot tell me his ABCs.

I hear a cry from one side of this nation to another that says, "I want to make a difference in this world. Will you show me how?" Well, I'm a simple person and I have always learned best by watching someone else, so would you let me tell you the simple story—my own—of one person who stepped out onto this mountain? My own story reflects what I believe: if God wrapped your package with a love or a talent, then that's what you take onto this mountain to change it. I had a love for kids and I had a talent for stories. Those were my two gifts to take onto this mountain. Yours will be different.

Twenty-one years ago, I was appointed to take over a youth center by a high school student of mine in the inner city. He had been elected to political office and was in charge of an exploding youth shelter where a boy hanged himself to death. My former student remembered his homeroom teacher from the inner city and Camden High School and asked me to take it over. So that's how I arrived.

. . . .

I learned from that experience that we had to change the atmosphere from an "us against them" attitude to a place where we would give the children the tools to succeed. The boys and girls who come into my center are teenage felons; there are no cream puffs here. They are children charged with murder, mayhem, drugs, prostitution—the ones that you lock your doors and pay big bucks for security systems to protect you from. These are my boys and girls.

So that was how I started, but I have to tell you, I was a pretty ordinary person. You have to get that clear in your head. It isn't going to be the psychiatrist or the mayor, or the senator that changes the mountain. It is going to be ordinary, unlikely people who step out to change it.

The Child of Violence

I will tell you the results of violence. In the 1940s when I lived in China, and in the 1990s with the children that I touch, the first protection is to become emotionally numb. You cannot keep looking at bayonets and hearing guns and seeing blood and writing about friends who have died until their names run off the page. . . .

So the child uses a technique called distancing. He pulls back into a safe place and sees it happening to somebody else. And the rage and the fright disappear in the cracks and crannies of a child's soul and may never come out again. The child is distancing, because you just can't keep feeling that level of pain.

"Spend Time with Me"

The first message is: Daddy, Mommy, spend time with me! Wrap me close to you with memories that I will never forget.

The answer from the children starts at that point. You want to change America? Get the stopwatch out in your own home and time how many seconds a day you spend talking with your children. Studies in America say the average working father and mother spend thirty seconds a day in meaningful communication with their children. Thirty seconds a day does not compete with a television that is on in the average American home for eight hours a day.

"Feed My Spirit"

I want to present you two children: Maria and Mary. Maria sat next to me, writing her story. Her headline was "Tall Mans, Fat Mans, Black Mans, White Mans, All Putting Tips in My Panty Strip."

I said "Little one! Child. Why did you run away from home in the first place?" She said, "My daddy called me freeloader at home. At the topless go-go bar, the mans call me Sweet Stuff." That is Maria.

And Mary stands in front of you this morning. I was fourteen years old the year I lost my hand in an accident. . . . My father was braiding my pigtails for me one day as I was getting ready for school and he said, "Mary, sweetheart, do you know what your little brother, Bertie, said to me when he heard that you lost your hand? Bertie said, 'Now Mary can't ride her bicycle.'" Well, I had a feeling my younger brother had his eye out on my new Raleigh bicycle with hand grips on it, and my daddy said, "Mary, sweetheart, do you know what I said to Bertie? I told him, 'I don't know why not.'"

I don't know why not. I have carried the banner of my father's words across my sky for over forty years. Not just the words, the believing in me. My daddy told me handicaps had nothing to do with what was on the outside of you. Handicaps were only on the inside. Mary Taylor was not handicapped.

Two little girls. Maria and Mary. I was the inheritor, but so was Maria. Our children speak to us: "Feed my spirit."

Case Study: A Challenge to the Cuban Church

Héctor Méndez, pastor, Presbyterian Church and General Secretary of YMCA, Havana, Cuba

The pastor was meeting with his long-range planning committee in the Protestant church in downtown Havana. All of the various ideas had advocates in the committee. Some people wanted no change. That was impossible because the country had changed. Some wanted a place to escape from the realities and difficulties they faced. Others wanted to become a social agency and provide for the needy and the elderly.

The pastor thought about all of the changes over the last forty years. The years were sometimes lean, and the people were sometimes anxious, but their role as a church had been defined for them. Now that they could make a decision, what would it be?

Revolutionary Times

Mr. López, the chair, reflected on past events for those who were new to the committee. He remembered how Dr. Fidel Castro, a young lawyer, became a legendary guerrilla fighter leading a group of farmers, workers, and students to victory: "When on January 1, 1959, the Cuban Revolution, under Castro's leadership, triumphed over a well-trained and well-equipped army, all the Cuban churches supported the changes made in the country. Little did we know that in a very short time the Cuban church would face a great challenge!

"In that first year, Protestant churches continued to be in favor of the Revolution, although some problems emerged between the revolutionary government and the Roman Catholic Church. This may have been, in part, because some revolutionary laws affected certain rich families who were large contributors to and supporters of the Catholic Church. Then, in 1961 when schools were nationalized, Protestant churches began to distance themselves from the revolutionary government."

Most of the members knew the rest of the history. In April 1961 when the Bay of Pigs invasion occurred, Castro defined the Cuban Revolution as a socialist revolution, inspired by Marxist-Leninist ideology. Little by little, Cuba began to feel the great influence of the Soviet Union. Education systems and other patterns from the Soviet way of life, including a strong atheistic element, were copied in Cuba. The ideological confrontation came at that time. Many pastors and lay leaders who had high positions in the Protestant churches decided to leave the country, going mainly to the United States.

A difficult and confusing situation emerged:
• congregations became only little groups of mostly elderly women;
• resources of all kinds became scarce;
• because of political discrimination designed to lead new generations away from God, few children and youth attended church.

Under this situation a small but faithful group remained in the Cuban churches. It was a hard time since there was a shortage of material resources and a general feeling of uncertainty about the future of the church. These Christians asked themselves: What perspective should the church have in a communist country like Cuba where the church role was limited to giving ritual assistance to a little group of faithful members?

Reverend Méndez, the pastor, continued: "Under these circumstances, the Cuban church accepted the challenge of being faithful to our Lord. For many years Cuban Christians tried to live the gospel and give testimonies of Jesus Christ. Those were hard times when Christians were seen as old-fashioned or as people who did not understand the Cuban revolutionary process.

"At that time we emphasized the Christian testimony; we asked our youth to be the best students; we asked our workers to be the best workers in every sector of Cuban life. As Christians, we gave our testimony that faith does not prevent us from standing for good ideas, even those that are opposed by leaders in power."

Years later, the results of those efforts became evident. Space for Christians began to be developed. Dr. Maria Aguirre, who chaired the missions committee, remembered the meeting in April 1990 between President Castro and a group of over seventy Christian leaders. To everyone's amazement, the meeting lasted more than four hours. "We told him of our interest in working in Cuba and in caring for the poor and sick. We wanted to contribute our gifts, not only in the spiritual way—a very important matter for us—but also in the social work in our country. Finally, President Castro recognized that Christians could help the country very much because of their moral and ethical values. But for that to happen, all kinds of discrimination had to be removed in schools and jobs.

"From then on, an opening began for the Cuban churches. It reached a new visibility with Pope John Paul II's visit in January 1998. However, it is important to realize that it was not Pope John Paul II who caused the mental changes in the Cuban revolutionary leaders, but the Cuban Christians who were faithful to the gospel for more than thirty years in spite of living in adverse conditions."

Everyone nodded. The Cuban church had accepted the challenge of being a small church in difficult times. Now it is called to accept the challenge of being a growing church. Members of the committee shared anecdotes that showed how God has used the believers in Cuba:

- Churches that previously had as few as eight to ten members now have crowded sanctuaries.
- In the 1970s, the Presbyterian camp had a capacity of thirty. Now it can serve 200 youth.
- Evangelical Theological Seminary in Matanzas, supported by the Methodist, Presbyterian, and Episcopal Churches, had only a few students in the 1970s and 1980s. In some years there may have been no graduates or only a single graduate. Now the seminary is full. Youth wait eagerly for the graduation of some students so they might enter. Recently, fifty laypersons graduated from a three-year course in theology. Of the fifty, half were women.
- New laity training programs are being developed in Havana.
- The Cuban church is using new musical rhythms in religious music. The scandal of using indigenous music is past. There are now many musical groups that are composing Cuban religious music.
- In the midst of the fiscal and material difficulties caused by the U.S. embargo and the collapse of socialism in Eastern Europe (which had provided most of Cuba's economic assistance), the churches in Cuba have accepted their role of cooperating in humanitarian aid. The Medical Commission of the Council of Churches in Cuba brings medi- cine and medical aid to hospitals. Caritas, a Roman Catholic organization, is doing similar work. Many Cuban churches have created commissions to assist elderly and needy people.
- There was a time when no Bibles, or few Bibles, were available, so that Cubans had to repair old Bibles continually. These Bibles were passed from hand to hand as things of value. Cuban Christians thank God that thousands of Bibles have been brought to Cuba through the cooperation of the United Bible Societies and the Bible Commission of the Council of Churches of Cuba. The Bibles are distributed throughout the country. In Cuba the Bible is the book everyone wants.

The committee sat in silence. How was all of this possible after almost forty years of living with an ideological struggle and an atheistic education? How could these Christians understand the wonderful reemergence of the Christian faith in a country that had declared itself Marxist-Leninist? Surely God had used the testimony of the faithful Cuban church. The Holy Spirit had guided the people, and now new possibilities were being realized with great success. Many prayers were being answered.

Rev. Méndez brought the committee back to the task at hand: "How can we face the new millennium with a church that will remain faithful while constantly growing?"

He read from the newsprint on the wall that held the opinions expressed in the earlier session:

We want to be a place of caring but not an escape or refuge in difficult times.

We want to care for the poor and needy but not become another social agency.

We want to have the same church with prayer and Bible studies that we had when were just little groups of Christians.

We want to be dedicated and dynamic and continue to grow.

The church, called to fulfill God's will, must be ready to accept the current challenges, both in easy and hard times. What was that special challenge Christ had for Cuba in this new era?

5. Our Engagement in Mission

Introduction

Recently a pastor entitled his sermon, "The Car's Not Empty." He began by relating an experience while returning a video to Blockbuster. He had one of his pugs with him on the front seat. The only parking place was on an incline, causing the dog to roll off to the floor, which was of no consequence, except the dog became invisible. As the pastor got out of the car, he used the appropriate hand motion and said to the dog, "Stay, stay." Another Blockbuster patron came by at that precise moment, stopped and stared, then said in amazement, "That's a new development. I still have to use the emergency brake!"

We often hear a criticism that The United Methodist Church is no longer in mission to the world, or that we have few caring mission personnel. Perhaps we are looking for one type of "passenger" and have missed the fact that the car is not empty.

I fear that some United Methodists think that there is a land where God is not, and that we, who are in mission, carry God, as if in a tote bag, to this remote place. Robert Harman and Edward Poitras both testify that this is not so. There is no place where God is not already at work. As United Methodists we understand this as God's prevenient and amazing grace at work.

Tex Sample testifies to the vitality of "apprenticeship" in mission, even in short-term volunteer mission. Lesslie Newbigin shows us that the field for evangelism is often at "home," even in the United States and Europe. Samuel Escobar shows us that often the most effective form for mission is from the margins to the margins, rather than from the rich to the poor or the powerful to the weak. Edward Poitras reminds us of the joy in serving the Lord.

Mission is not someone else's job. It is ours—yours and mine. God calls each of us by name. May we have the courage to respond as Isaiah did, "Here am I; send me!"

Learning by Apprenticeship

Tex Sample, Professor of Church and Society, Saint Paul School of Theology, Kansas City, Missouri

Excerpted from *Ministry in an Oral Culture: Living with Will Rogers, Uncle Remus & Minnie Pearl* (Louisville, Ky.: Westminster John Knox Press, 1994), 16-19.

When Peggy and I left Millsaps College for me to go to seminary at Boston University, we found the Northeast to be radically different from our Mississippi roots. I remember going to the largest supermarket in the area to ask if they had grits. The clerk told me I would have to go to a hardware store!

We greatly missed the local food of Mississippi. We particularly missed those magnificent icebox rolls that Peggy's mother made. They were the kind of rolls you had to chew real fast before they simply melted in your mouth.

One night in Boston I told Peggy how much I loved her mother's icebox rolls and how much I missed them.

"Well, why don't we call her and ask for the recipe?"

"Oh, do you suppose she would let us have it?" I asked, sensitive to the fact that sometimes recipes are like mystery religions and their possessors guard them closely.

"Well, let's try," Peggy said.

When we called, her mother seemed genuinely touched by our appreciation for her culinary art and indicated she would send the recipe the next day. When it arrived, it said this:

Pour some flour in the bottom of a bowl
Put in a dash of baking soda
Add a pinch of salt.
Pour in some milk.
Stir it until it looks right
Bake it to a honey brown.

Stymied, we called her on the phone again. "We are thrilled to get the recipe," I said, trying to sound as appreciative as I really was, but also not wanting to be affrontive about the fact that the unspecific nature of her recipe was not adequately helpful. "We do have a few questions," I went on. "You say, 'put some flour in the bottom of a bowl.' Uh, how much flour?"

"Well, it depends on how many rolls you want to make," she answered with more than a hint of frustration.

"I see . . . okay . . . uh, how much . . . is . . . a . . . dash?"

"Well," she said, moving from frustration toward exasperation, "a dash is a dash. *Everybody* knows what a dash is."

"Of course," I answered, now attempting to placate her and wondering how and why I ever got myself into this spot with my mother-in-law of less than a year. Trying now to appear as less than the bumbling ignoramus I felt myself to be, I tried covering my over-exposure with the weak line: *"and a pinch is a pinch."*

"What else would it be?" she said, with a sense for the reality of things that at that moment seemed to have evaded *me* all my life.

"Look, Tex, this isn't working," she said as she put an end to this ritualized blood-letting of my dignity. "You wait until you two come home this summer, and I will take you into my kitchen. Then, I'll *show* you how to make icebox rolls."

That following summer, as she apprenticed us on the making of icebox rolls, I realized that she could never have conveyed her art to us through the literal framework of a recipe. Too many things were going on for her to capture them on a written page.

I learned then that traditional/oral people do not learn by "study," but through apprenticeship. . . . My guesstimate is that half the people in the churches are like this. It may be that, in regard to their lives in the church, the percentage is even higher because many people were raised in the church, and an oral approach to things religious was set early and remains so.

Considerations like these have led me to ask questions about the literate cast of a good deal of church programming. If young people and adults are basically oral in their approach to life, and they continually find themselves in churches that are literate, these folk will not likely continue to come. As anyone who knows much about the church understands, many people who will come to church when there is something to do—paint a room, rebuild a wall, cook a supper, provide volunteer time for a community service—will not come to a Sunday school class or to worship. I have always been struck by the number of youth who will come to Scouts, with its strong apprenticeship and merit badge approach, but who will not come to Sunday school. Moreover, most of the adult Sunday school classes that are really effective with people out of the lower sixty percent of the class structure are far more likely to be communal gatherings with a wide range of practices, socials, and service projects for the group than "classes" for study as such. Please understand, I am certainly not opposed to, but rather actively support, people who want to study the faith and mission of the church. My point, instead, is that this is not indigenous to the lives of a majority of people in the United States.

For these reasons I think a significant part of the ministry and mission of our churches needs to be done in an apprenticeship way. The Sunday school needs options that are oriented around learning from church members while carrying out the ministry and mission of the church. . . .

For traditional/oral people much is to be learned in the teaching that occurs through hands-on mission. For example, Habitat for Humanity is a significant program because its mission clearly has a theological and faith purpose and meaning, and because for a good many, participation involves learning on the job. So much of our work in the church involves teaching people about the faith and then asking how this can be implemented. Certainly an enormous opportunity awaits those who learn in apprenticeship roles where faith issues arise and need to be addressed in the active work of discipleship.

Mission from the Margins to the Margins

Samuel Escobar, teaches missiology, Eastern Baptist Theological Seminary, Philadelphia, Pennsylvania, and theological education in Lima, Peru

Excerpted from "Mission from the Margins to the Margins: Two Case Studies from Latin America," *Missiology: An International Review* (January 1998): 87-94.

How does mission take place when the missionary vocation rises among people who live in the margins of society and not in the mainstream? Important segments of Hispanic minorities in the United States, for instance, live in the margins of American life, but I see among them signs of missionary vitality. How do people from those margins of society engage in Christian mission at a global level today? Mission history might be helpful for a start.

. . . .

When we consider the missionary stories of the New Testament, we have to agree that they also are simple stories about simple people. The fact that today they are part of the living memory of many human beings does not change the simplicity of the stories and the characters. They were from humble beginnings indeed. From time to time we need to be reminded of that fact, especially when we experience what experts call "a change of paradigms." When the apostle Paul traveled from city to city in Asia Minor, chroniclers, poets, and consultant-philosophers of the emperors—the journalists of those days—did not see anything important about him that would be worth recording. It was people who shared his faith who took the trouble to keep a record of events and to save his correspondence. He was a strong personality and a man with leadership ability, no doubt, but that was it. He was marginal in the great "historical events" of his time.

The paradigm that is ending is the colonial paradigm of "important" missionaries as representatives of the highly civilized and developed world taking a downward mobility trip to civilize and evangelize poor natives in faraway places. That was mission from above, from a position of power, progress, and prestige. In many places now, willingly or unwillingly, mission has to be carried on "from below," from positions of vulnerability, lack of political protection, and scarcity of funds. I know Peruvians of Japanese descent who have gone to Japan to make some money doing the "dirty" jobs that no Japanese wants to do. They live in marginal areas of the main cities. They went because they had to go; their economic survival was at stake. However, also they see their presence in Japan as a form of mission, and it is mission "from below."

Maybe this type of experience is motivating us to rediscover the marginality of the New

Testament Christians and missionaries and the recurrence of that paradigm in several moments of history. Much has been said about capitalist upper- or middle-class Americans who went as missionaries to Latin America, armed with their diplomas, their money, their diplomatic letters of presentation, and their ideology of Manifest Destiny. For a balanced view, it is worth exploring other cases and other stories. Some missionaries left the margins of society in their missionary base and followed the call to the margins of society in the mission land. The actors were simple people, migrants, factory workers, members of sects, experienced in religious persecution and socially or religiously marginal—simple people in simple places. However, they have left marks in the spiritual history of the countries to which they went, and they continue to influence the communities they founded.

In 1909, Adolf Gunnar Vingren (1879-1933), a Baptist minister, and his friend Daniel Berg (1884-1963), a steel worker, both Swedes, had pentecostal experiences in South Bend, Indiana, and their friend Olaf Uldin prophesied that they were going to be missionaries in a place called "Pará." "The two went to a library and began to search all the maps of the world until they found a state in Brazil called Pará. Taking this to be an indication of the Lord's will, the two set out."[1]

It was as simple as that. It was not the world of mission boards, strategies, and master plans. It is easy to forget how much American missionary work during our century has been done through this combination of religious fervor, faith in a vision from God, and readiness to move; volunteerism is the most important ingredient of mission history. . . . From the religious margins of American society, a disorganized and unconventional missionary movement was taking place. Historians have had difficulty recording it or paying attention to it even though in more than one place it had a surprising success.[2]

Having come from the hardships of marginality in Sweden and migration in Chicago, it was not difficult for Vingren and Berg to adopt a self-supporting missionary style, to mix with the common folk and to live with them. . . . Not having a long-established ecclesiastical tradition, they gave more freedom to the Brazilian converts to find organizational patterns and evangelistic methodologies that were contextual. . . . Berg and Vingren reached the bottom of the social scale and allowed the birth of a church that could be wholly contextual in its social environment. This church has grown to become the largest national body of Assemblies of God in the world.

This story of simple people coming from the experience of marginality in their own country and going to work among marginalized people in marginal geographical areas have many lessons for us today as we think of what it means to do mission from below. They correspond to what Orlando Costas called "a model of contextual evangelization from the periphery."³ Costas's understanding of his own contemporary context emphasized that "evangelization should be geared first and foremost to the nations' peripheries, where the multitudes are found and where the Christian faith has always had the best opportunity to build a strong base."⁴

Mission Evangelization in Secular Societies

Lesslie Newbigin, before his death in 1998, was a major influence in ecumenical missions for more than fifty years; a minister in the United Reformed Church (UK) and former bishop in the Church of South India

Excerpted from *A Word in Season* (Grand Rapids: Eerdmans, 1994), 150-57.

The secular societies that have developed in Europe since the seventeenth century share the common belief that reliable knowledge about human nature is to be found not by reliance upon divine revelation and grace but by reliance upon the methods of empirical science. This, broadly speaking, is the dogma that controls public life, as distinct from the private opinions that individuals are free to hold.

. . . .

The "secular" society is not a neutral area into which we can project the Christian message. It is an area already occupied by other gods. We have a battle on our hands. We are dealing with principalities and powers. What, then, is evangelism in this context?

To our "secular" contemporaries the answer to this question is quite simple. The Christian church is a voluntary association of people who wish to promote certain "values" for themselves and for society. These "values," like all others, are matters of personal choice. They are not matters of "fact" that everyone has to accept. It follows that the success of these "values" depends on the number of people who support them. There is a diminishing number of people who identify themselves with the Christian churches. The churches are therefore in danger of collapsing. Evangelism is an effort by the churches to avert this collapse and to recruit more adherents to their cause. . . .

The first evangelism in the New Testament is the announcement by Jesus that the kingdom of God is at hand. This, if one may put it so, is not church news, but world news. It requires an immediate response in action. There is immediate excitement. People flock to hear. . . . What seemed to be the end is the new beginning. The tomb is empty, Jesus is risen, death is conquered, God does reign after all. There is an explosion of joy, news that cannot be kept secret. Everyone must hear it. A new creation has begun. One does not have to be summoned to the "task" of evangelism. If these things are really true, they have to be told.

That, I suppose, is why St. Paul did not have to remind his readers about the duty of evangelism.

. . . .

I would suggest that in thinking of evangelism in a secular society, the following five points may be helpful.

1. Evangelism is not the effort of Christians to increase the size and importance of the church. It is sharing the good news that God reigns—good news for those who believe, bad news for those who reject. . . . God reigns and his reign is revealed and effective in the incarnation, ministry, death, and resurrection of Jesus. . . .

2. The clue to evangelism in a secular society must be the local congregation. There are many other things of which one could speak—mass evangelism, Christian literature, radio and television, and so on. These are auxiliary. Many of them can be very valuable. But they are auxiliary to the primary center of evangelism, which is the local congregation. The congregation should live by the true story and center their life in the continual remembering and relating of the true story. . . .

3. It will be a major part of the work of such congregations to train and enable members to act as agents of the kingdom in the various sectors of public life where they work. . . .

4. From this it follows that it will also be the task of the local congregation to equip members to enter into this dialogue, to explain the Christian story and its bearing on daily life. And of course the explanation will not be complete without the invitation to become part of the community. . . .

5. If this approach is right, evangelism is not just the call to personal conversion, although it is that. It is not just a program for church growth, although it is that also. It is not just preaching, although it is that, and it is not just action for changing society, although it is that too. . . . It is possible to envision a society in which Christians have engaged so seriously over several decades with the consequences of the Enlightenment (good and bad) and with the kind of society that has developed at the end of the twentieth century that those who achieve the highest standards of excellence in all the sectors of public life—politics, industry, learning, and the arts—may be shaped in their public work by the Christian story. Then the worship of the triune God as he is made known to us in Jesus may again be the focus of ordinary life in our towns and villages.

The Global Nature of the Church

Robert J. Harman, Deputy General Secretary, serving in the areas of Evangelization and Church Growth, and Community and Institutional Ministries, General Board of Global Ministries, New York, New York

Excerpted from "Challenges of Mission in the Post Cold War Context," in *Mission and Transformation in a Changing World* (New York: General Board of Global Ministries, 1998), 1-14. This essay is based on a lecture delivered at Iliff Theological Seminary, January 29, 1997.

Cultural differences, which are God's creative gifts to a world community, are not to be seen as the unequivocal cause of enmity or conflict between peoples and nations. There is an opportunity in this post-Cold War period to develop new models for interethnic understanding and interaction. Let us seize it.

. . . .

There is more to being a global church than linking together communities of faith with purely local or tribal origins. A global church seeks to understand, appreciate, celebrate, and tolerate a host of differences, while faithfully following the requirements of a life in covenant aimed at making a qualitative difference in the world. The church of Jesus Christ is the whole body of Christ in each and every place. In all cultural contexts, the revelation of Christ occurs with genuinely distinctive characteristics, so the church in each place is honored and respected. A global denominational (or dare we say "tribal") identity that settles for cultural homogenization would be something less than a full and vital expression of Christ's church.

To be "global" is the objective of every enterprise in today's growing market economy. Showing the signs of a "global" awareness by making experimental forays into less familiar regions of the world is one thing. Making a contribution to a lasting difference in the development of a truly global and fully human community is quite another.

Not just globalization but "glocalization," a term some religious thinkers use to express cultural sensitivity, should be the aim of world mission for The United Methodist Church in this period. To create a variation of a familiar slogan, we must "think globally, but remember to pray locally," recognizing that people who pray anywhere these days must have the whole world in their thoughts.

. . . .

To return to Wesley's mission statement, the task of the churches is "reforming the nations, especially the churches." To be reformers today, the churches must enter the public square in spite of a strong trend toward specializing in the private sphere. The churches must help frame the ethical dimensions of the struggle for human security and well-being in the all-important global context.

The prophet Isaiah (chapter 65) offers a vision of what the reign of God would look like in our temporal economy. We are familiar with its imagery of the lamb and the lion lying in peaceful repose, but there is more to commend it to our consideration. The farmer's labors in planting crops would be rewarded by his having enough for his family to eat. The builder of a house would be blessed with its shelter. The young would grow into old age and the old live in peace. Underlying this vision is not the practice of politics or economics as we know those disciplines today. They are succeeding only in producing a world order in which most people are ill-fed, ill-housed, ill-clothed, undereducated, and prey to preventable conflicts and diseases. Isaiah's vision is built upon a moral substructure of basic values and virtues—especially distributive and communicative justice—that inform and shape the significance of human individuals.

The late Russian theologian Nikolai Berdyaev found in the hunger for distributive justice the occasion for a deepening spirituality. "The question of bread for myself is a material question, but the question of bread for my neighbor, for everybody, is a spiritual question. Man does not live by bread alone, but he does live by bread, and there should be bread for all. Society should be organized so that there is bread for all, and then it is that the spiritual question will present itself before all men (humanity) in all its depth."[5]

Is The United Methodist Church, in wanting to be a global church, prepared to wrestle with the spiritual questions that have bread-and-butter consequences—not only for its own organizational life but for the life of the world? In our concern for a global church let us not focus too much upon structure and the organizational issues of membership and participation. Membership has its privileges, but a global church will accept responsibility for global citizenship.

Joy in Receiving

Edward W. Poitras, Professor Emeritus, World Christianity, Perkins School of Theology, Dallas, Texas and for 35 years, missionary in Korea

Excerpted from "Joy in Receiving: A Reflection on Mission Motive and Modality," in *Missiology: An International Review* (October 1995): 387-99.

Joy seems to be one of the most neglected aspects of the Christian life, especially in theological discourse. Mission thinking is no exception, yet I believe joy to be a central reality in mission. The problem is not merely an oversight. It is evident that a good many persons engaged in mission seem deficient in the quality of joy. Protestations of joy in believing have sometimes been ironically belied by negativity, severity, and even cruelty.

The failure of some missionaries and their followers to exhibit the joyful abundance of life which the gospel promises remains one of the strangest ironies of mission. Furthermore, in a world often depicted as close to the brink of self-destruction, when visions of the end abound, it might seem almost irresponsible to speak of joy in the midst of so much evil and suffering.

Joy and Suffering

The question of suffering in relation to joy is important for mission for at least three reasons: (1) Christian mission has been understood as a response to the world's suffering, (2) suffering has often accompanied the conversion of persons in cultures shaped by other religious traditions, and (3) missionary witness has often been seen as a heroic venture calling for sacrificial suffering.

Mission as a response to suffering. Although Christian mission throughout history has responded to suffering, missionaries have often failed to find joy in situations of human misery. Especially when mission has been a service for the poor by the rich, suffering has been seen as the antithesis of joy. But as Gustavo Gutiérrez learned from a poor woman in Lima, "suffering is not the opposite of joy; sadness and worse still, bitterness, are the opposite of joy."[6] It is the poor who first understand that there can be joy even in the midst of suffering, notably that joy which comes through solidarity in resisting forces of destruction and repression.

. . . .

Christian mission must respond to suffering as an evil to be overcome, but missionary witnesses are mistaken when they think that joy must be imported into situations of suffering, when it is more likely to emerge from within them.

Suffering resulting from conversion. Mission practice has often involved calling people to conversions that result in ostracism. In the case of so-called ancestor worship in China, Korea, and Japan, missionaries often advocated confrontations with established beliefs that resulted in intense suffering, especially for new believers and their families. This pain was seen as the cost of casting aside their former ways.

Christian mission, then, has often led to pain rather than joy, and this irony has not been lost on believers of other faiths. When that suffering has not been informed by joy, as it was in New Testament missionary witness, we have a failure to grasp the heart of the gospel, complicated by a confusion of gospel and culture.

Mission as sacrificial suffering. The imposition of cultural discontinuity seems related to the ideal of sacrificial missionary service, where hardship and suffering are seen as evidence of valid mission. Of course, persecution and suffering for the sake of authentic gospel witness were experienced by Jesus, then Stephen, Paul, and many others in the New

Testament. Such has been the lot of many missionaries since. Yet joy shines through in the biblical record of missionary witness, even when suffering has followed.

Motives in Mission

Mission as obedience. A helpful way to relate joy to mission is by considering missionary motivations. Undoubtedly, the most common has been obedience to the great commission summarized in Matthew 28:18-20. The Lord has said, "Go," so the missionary's duty is to obey.

Dutiful obedience can easily squelch the quality of joy. Missionary communities are familiar with the figure often caricatured by novelists: the dour, driven person who has neither time nor inclination to pause for smelling flowers. I have seen seasoned missionaries who made life miserable for colleagues, and who tried to reproduce the same harsh mentality in those they taught or led.

. . . .

The cross can be seen as the pained, loving heart of God. Only then can we be assured that the healing of the victims of sin is embraced together with the repentance of the perpetrators of evil. Joy is possible, then, because God has shown that suffering can be borne, absorbed, and transmuted within an unshakable affirmation of the goodness and value of life.

Mission as alleviation of human need. Another important mode of mission coheres around the motive of responding to human need. The missioner helps bring about the world God intends. Love is often the dominant motive in this form of mission. We share the love which has come through Jesus Christ; we seek to make known God's love of all the world.

In missionary practice, however, this motive and its service can succumb to a flatness and a joylessness that follow from sensing the overwhelming scale of evil and human need. This is the mission modality in which burnout and breakdown seem most likely to occur. . . .

Hidden doubts about ability to cope with huge challenges are surely a reason for withdrawal from fields of service. Many missionaries withdraw while remaining at their posts, however, by limiting social contacts, absorbing themselves in hobbies or the expatriate community. My personal experience includes times of near-burnout resulting from overload and a sense of depletion in the face of constant demands for self-giving.

. . . .

Mission as response to God in the world. It is possible to follow H. Richard Niebuhr's suggestion and consider mission as a form of response.[7] Mission becomes one form of response, perhaps the primary response, to the presence and activity of God in the world. . . .

This has two advantages over other familiar forms. First, it fosters the attitude of mission in joy, for it locates the motive and energy of mission in a liberation received from Christ, neither in obedience to a command nor in the need of the recipient. Second, it opens the way to mutuality in mission.

Mission as an expression of joy. The joy of a realized, mature selfhood is a pervading stance, more enduring than particular feelings, knowledge, or confessions of faith. Joy will be the fitting response to the presence and activity of God in the world. Joy enables the endearing quality of humor, reflecting a balanced view of self and an accurate sense of what has enduring value. It is, I believe, the discovery of joy as a motive that distinguishes those missionaries who witness effectively.

Both critical awareness and social analysis have developed to a point where we can never hope to regain the lost innocence of earlier, even modern times. Mission based upon joy transcends analyses of thought, culture, and human need, yet takes these seriously as it engages the world. A mission response to the poor, for example, ceases to be a burden (or technological program) carried by the dutiful rich, becoming instead a release, when we understand that the poor are empowered and the rich freed from greed, liberated together to resolve shared systemic problems.

Mission Is Giving and Receiving

If mission is understood as a sharing of liberation and joy with others, then the giver also is, and remains, a receiver. The attitude of grateful receiving from God can become the basis of mission, including a receptive and grateful attitude toward the creation and those to whom witness is made.

It is only natural to understand mission as an outward-directed activity. Mission began as a reaching out by the early Christian community, and it appears that scant attention was given to the standpoint of the hearers of the gospel. . . . Despite its early missionary adjustments to varied cultures, the church, especially in the West, consistently saw its missionary activity as an outward expansion from the center.

As a corrective, I suggest viewing mission from the standpoint of the recipients. In this way mission is seen first and foremost as an act of receiving. This is not to abandon the outgoing act of missionary giving. Missionary witness remains the same reality, but is seen in a more comprehensive light.

A New Approach

It has often been argued that mission must begin with listening and responding to people "where they are," so as to respond to them "on their terms" for the sake of "effective communication." What I am suggesting is more radical. The missionary must first assume the standpoint of the recipient and attempt to understand witness as it is being heard and seen.

This is not merely incorporating sensitivity into an outward-moving missionary attitude, but the abandonment of that stance, instead bringing active missionary witness within the context of the receiver's stance.

. . . .

Mission thus becomes an invitation to join God's household of joy. To the extent that a linear, outward-directed concept of mission can be modified or abandoned, it will be better to think of mission as a response to God's grace throughout the creation. . . . In this kind of image, mission spreads with softer edges, while the acts of receiving and giving are seen more clearly as a single reality.

Case Study: "A Church for All People?"

Garnett E. Foster

Excerpted from *Journal for Case Teaching* 5 (Fall 1993): 95-97. Copyright © The Case Study Institute. All names have been disguised to protect the privacy of the individuals involved.

The heavily accented voice on the telephone was full of anger and hurt: "I have to tell you as my pastor how the church has failed me. No one cares that my mother died and that right after I returned from her funeral in Africa, my uncle and an infant niece died. No one except you and two friends came to be with me. Others just called and asked me to do a job. They didn't even express any feeling. They just see me as someone who can work for the church. What is the church for if not to be with you when you are grieving?"

For two years Bruce Derr had been pastor of a two-hundred-fifty-member church in a suburb bordering a major east coast city. International organizations and multinational corporations as well as immigration for political and economic reasons had brought an influx of people to the area from around the world. Seventy primary languages were spoken in the neighborhood high school. The church reflected this diversity; thirty percent of its members came from eighteen different nations.

The challenge of this diversity was the key reason Bruce had accepted the call to become pastor of the congregation. Having had experience overseas, he was captured by the church's expressed vision of its ministry: "A Church for All People." A large sign in front of the church building and the congregation's publications made public this mission. The highlight of the year was World Communion Sunday when persons from numerous nations gathered around the communion table in dress from their country, leading in prayer in their own language. He saw this as a foretaste of God's reign where people would gather from north and south, from east and west, and sit at table together.

But Bruce knew it was only a foretaste. He remembered the friction caused by this diversity. Several of the more liberated professional women were indignant at the flirty, macho way Latin American men related to them. At every Worship Committee meeting there was heated discussion over the hymns to be used in worship. Many of the international folks from missionary backgrounds wanted to sing hymns such as "Onward Christian Soldiers" that they had used in worship at home. But the militaristic tunes and words of such hymns contradicted the understanding of the gospel held by many from a more liberal American tradition.

Those from the dominant culture were quick to express their displeasure in public meetings or through letters to the editor of the church's newsletter. But those from other nations were hesitant to express discomfort with the congregation's ways of functioning except in private conversations with Bruce.

Bruce was pleased with some of the ways lay leaders had sought to deepen communication between persons from different cultures, often incorporating the gifts of each into the corporate life of the congregation. Members from Ghana led worship at the church picnic, involving the congregation in an experience that had been an annual event for them "at home." Forums explored the experience of members from various nations, emphasizing both life in the country of origin and the difficulties of living in the United States.

In spite of some progress in becoming a church for all people, Bruce knew that on a day-to-day basis upper middle-class white professionals ran the church. They did business with good process skills and great efficiency. Yet the task was usually more important than persons. He had encouraged the Nominating Committee to make certain that the diversity of the congregation was represented on the governing body and committees of the church. The chair of the committee reported back that she had tried to recruit nominees from all the nationalities in the church, but most of those approached had reluctantly declined, stating they worked two jobs and had little time for church activities other than worship.

The telephone call had shattered Bruce's positive feelings and heightened his awareness that the differences in cultural norms and expectations within the congregation were deep and divisive. He knew they had to be named and dealt with. The caller, Ansa, was one of the Africans who had made time to serve on the governing body of the congregation and had been instrumental in establishing a sister parish in Nicaragua. He could name several members of the congregation for whom Ansa had been an important person in their faith journey.

Although he had a tendency to personalize the congregation's problems, Bruce knew that this was the governing body's challenge. During the time for sharing of concerns at the monthly meeting of the twelve members of the Council, he told of his conversation. "She expected the congregation to stand with her in her grieving, and few of us took time to reach out to her. She is angry that people had called inviting her to come to meetings and do things. She saw this as blatant insensitivity to her grieving. She feels her church had failed to meet her spiritual needs."

The Council responded with a stunned silence to Bruce's description of the conversation with Ansa. Susan broke the silence, quietly remembering: "Ansa was one of the few church members who called me when I was angry and chose not to come to church for a month. She cared enough to seek me out. It hurts that she felt I failed her." Fred responded: "I need the deep spirituality and concern for marginal people that Ansa adds to our deliberations." But sympathy and concern turned to frustration at not understanding Ansa's feelings.

Ruth, somewhat defensively, declared, "When I asked Ansa to do some work on the Mission Committee, I meant that invitation to be a caring way of inviting her to resume activity in the congregation and of reorienting her to 'normal' life." Ann told of the discomfort she had felt on the death of her father when an African member of the congregation had come to her house and "just sat" for hours. "I felt responsible for entertaining her, and her presence soon became a burden."

Bruce was aware of his own confusion as he watched the self-assurance of the governing body crumble under the honest expression of Ansa's pain and unmet expectations. He was haunted by the theory that was predominant in his denomination: only churches that are homogeneous can be "successful" growing churches. He believed firmly that diversity was a gift of God, and that God called diverse people into community, called them together to be the body of Christ in the world. But was it possible to be "A Church for All People"—or were the church growth experts right?

Study Guide for New Wineskins

The Spirit and Forms of Mission

Study Guide

The Spirit and Forms of Mission

You have been chosen to lead this study. What an honor! Through an individual or committee invitation, God has called you to help others reflect on the nature and mission of the church. You are not alone. This study book is a compilation of thoughts from several persons who have been asked to do the same.

Leading this class may be a new experience for you, or it may be one experience of many. Either way, the best way to begin is to prepare yourself for the task. Read the book. Understand the perspective of the various authors. Think how pictures show different aspects of an event depending on where the photographer is standing.

The same is true here. The call to ministry and mission may vary, depending on the country, race, gender, and economic context from which an individual speaks. Some writers are on the frontline in mission projects; some are ministers, teachers, and professors; some are missionaries, and some carry particular responsibility in their vocation for mission. All are committed to Christ and his church.

Have some questions in mind as you approach your reading. What is mission? How does God call us through Scripture? When and where does the world call out for love and compassion? What can I do? What would Jesus do? What is the best plan of action for my local church? Is there a special missional role for The United Methodist Church? How do we gain a truly global perspective? Where will the Spirit lead us in the next millennium?

As an anthology of writings about mission, the articles can be read in sections and in sequence. They also stand alone. It may be tempting to do a "quick read" of all of the articles. To do so may be to miss the depth and breadth of meaning. As an alternative (or as a second step), read and savor one article each day as part of a devotional time. It will take only a few minutes of disciplined time, and the efforts will be rewarding.

Begin with prayer. Read one selection. As you meditate, ask yourself what that reading suggests about the nature of God, our human situation, and how God in Christ is calling us to care for one another. Where do particular issues touch your life personally? Keep a pencil and paper nearby for recording feelings, insights, and possibilities. Use a shorthand way of seeing the interrelationships by using intertwining circles like the ones shown on the following page.

Model - to chart the many forms of mission

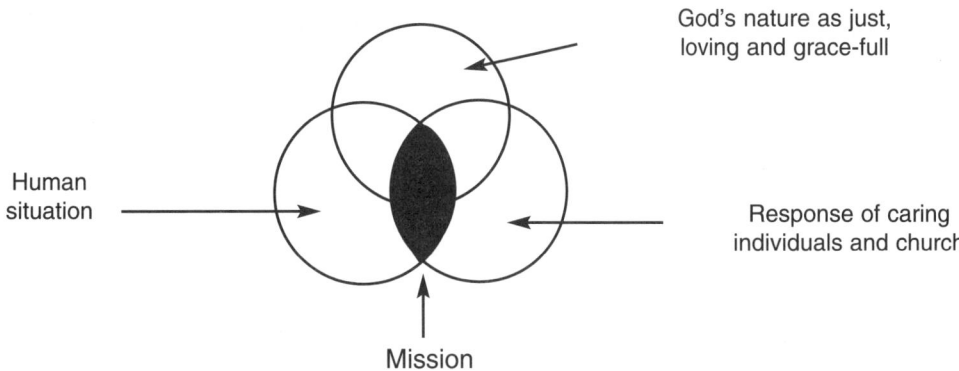

Example: 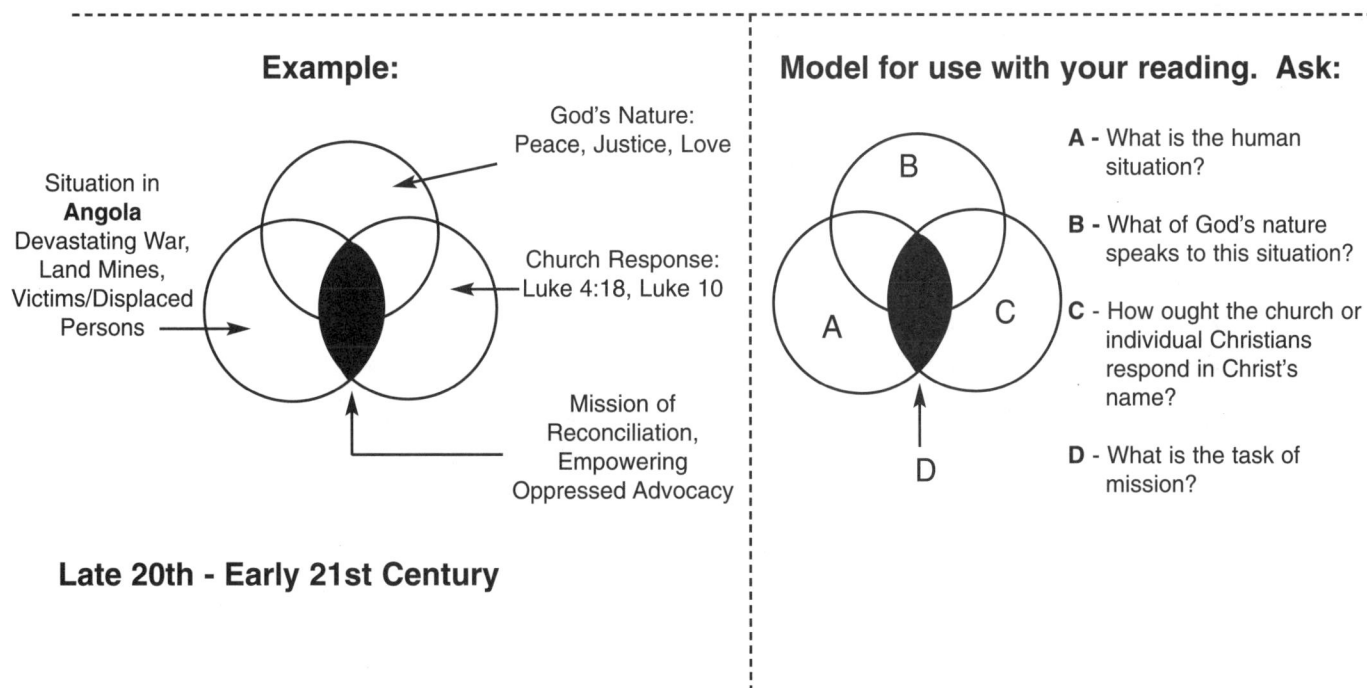 **Model for use with your reading. Ask:**

A - What is the human situation?

B - What of God's nature speaks to this situation?

C - How ought the church or individual Christians respond in Christ's name?

D - What is the task of mission?

Late 20th - Early 21st Century

From time to time, look over your notes to see how the subject and context of mission may have affected your response.

If possible, contact class members before the first session. This can be done by letter or phone. Encourage them to read the text in advance, and to bring with them a symbol of an exciting form of mission from their congregation. If all class members are from the same church, ask them to bring a symbol of a form of mission in which they have personally participated.

Planning the Class Session

In my experience, after we leaders have prepared *ourselves* to lead, then we can plan the actual sessions for the class. This study guide will list several options from which to choose. Do not attempt to do them all. Likewise, do not feel compelled to cover every subject that is mentioned in the book. Either alternative will make class participants feel overwhelmed and will lead to inaction rather than productive response.

The list of challenges for the twenty-first century can seem endless. For a class to feel responsible for every issue could lead to a missional paralysis in which both our courage and will to act are frozen. Therefore, it is important not to paint such a negative picture of the world that class members feel defeated before they begin. Rather, assist the class in discovering the areas of mission most important to them, and encourage them to join hands with sisters and brothers in Christ to change the dynamics of a particular situation and tend to the brokenness they find.

Each class session needs to have variety within it. Dick Murray has said, "Teaching may be defined as stimulating and enabling involvement with information to influence results."[1] Involvement means more than listening to words. It may mean using creative activities: role playing, case studies, music, and sharing of stories. These are ways of engaging the information through participation and personal experience. Additional ways include reflections and discussions on the readings, panel presentations, and videos.

"Worshipful work" is Charles Olsen's term that refers to the acknowledgment of the worship and inspiration that accompanies the "work" we do in and for the church. It means more than "bookend" prayers that begin and close our time together. It may mean a short worship time to center our thoughts. It always includes the presence of God's Spirit being symbolically and visibly demonstrated, usually with a lighted candle. It is what Murray refers to as "trust." We trust that God is present and active within the class and within each person in the group. Therefore, a recognition of that trust is appropriate.

We live in a world of images. Images are the dominant force in media. Some twenty-five years ago, Harvey Cox voiced a concern that those responsible for religious education "live and work on tiny rafts of written pages adrift in an ocean of images." How ironic! As people of faith, it ought to be easy to return to images and symbols that have been a part of our journey.

As a part of the "worshipful work," create a space for symbols. In each session, there will be suggestions for symbols—of our world, our faith, and our call to mission. If you are teaching away from your "home" setting, you may want to choose only one or two symbols each time and ask a local person to provide them for the class. The class sessions are not dependent on the symbols, but if you take the time to use them, you will find your class sessions are enriched. Remember, this is not an altar but a place where our eyes can see a symbol and our hearts remember that Christ is present in our learning and in our deliberation.

Creating this sacred space for study includes music. From our beginnings with the Wesleys, Methodists have put their theology in song. It is also true of our mission. Sociologists tell us that every major social movement has had a theme song. Therefore, as you plan this study, use a variety of music that lets the class examine its theology of mission and its belief that God calls persons from around the world to be in mission around the world.

Case studies may also be a new form of education to you. Sometimes we create situations for simulations and role plays. These can be helpful, and yet they are sometimes treated lightly because they are "pretend" situations. Case studies are useful because they are based on real-life situations. If this is a new method for you, please read Alan Neely's article carefully. Although four case studies are included, with limited class time you may want to choose one or two that have the most meaning for the class you are leading.

Benediction literally means "good word" (*bene*-good, *diction*-word). As you close each session, consider what good word can be given. Perhaps the "word" is a song, a liturgy, a prayer, a blessing, or a challenge. Send class members forth with this good word.

Overview of Sessions

The components of your class time include:
- Worshipful Work
- Learning through Involvement
- Information and Discussion
- Community Response
- Benediction

In a two-hour class, the time might be allocated like this:
- 0:00-0:15 Worshipful Work
- 0:15-1:05 Learning through Involvement
- 1:05-1:35 Information
- 1:35-1:55 Community Response
- 1:55-2:00 Benediction

The order might be changed and the three middle parts interspersed; for example, some "information" might be inserted in the midst of the "involvement." This schedule will assist you in allowing adequate time for active and experiential learning.

Materials needed:
- Bibles (a few extra for those who arrive without one)

- United Methodist Hymnals
- *Global Praise* (If these are not available in quantity, write to the General Board of Global Ministries for permission to copy any song you plan to use in the sessions.)
- *Prayer Calendar*
- *New World Outlook* and *Response* magazines
- Video spots from United Methodist Communications (nos. 5462, 5463, 5464)
- Candle and symbols for "Worshipful Work"
- Newsprint and markers

Your task, as leader, is to continually assess the engagement of the class, to provide multiple approaches to the material, and to invite or evoke responses to the spirit and forms of mission.

An Approach to Case Studies
Alan Neely

Excerpted from *Christian Mission: A Case Study Approach* (Maryknoll, N.Y.: Orbis, 1995), 3-18.

Case studies are not new. The story told to King David by the prophet Nathan (2 Samuel 12:1-14) about the rich man who had many flocks and herds but who, when an unexpected guest arrived, took a poor man's only ewe lamb in order to serve the guest, is a cleverly disguised and skillfully utilized case study. The king, as the prophet expected, entered into the case discussion with passion and indignation.

Likewise Plato's dialogues are examples of case studies in which Socrates engages the youth of Athens in philosophical discussions designed to establish universal truths. The philosopher asks questions and more questions. Whether discovering a point by a process of systematic doubt or by subjecting one's reasoning to a group critique, dialectical conversation is still valid, even when a unanimous resolution to a dilemma is not forthcoming.

. . . .

A case is a carefully written description of an actual situation or event fraught with ambiguity in which a person or persons must make a decision based upon the information at hand. . . . The data included are those factors that appear to be significant to the participant through whose eyes the case is written, but enough data are provided to allow the students to enter vicariously into the situation. Usually, though not always, a case is left open-ended. . . . In a case discussion the challenge to the student is to enter into the experience, face the dilemma, and imagine himself or herself as the decision-maker.

. . . .

Following the suggested steps will not only enable a student to enter the case authentically, but also to look forward to the discussion with excitement and anticipation.

Step 1: *Read the case.* Begin by reading the case quickly and getting a feel for what is happening. Note how the case begins. From whose perspective is the case written? Remember that a case describes a difficult problem for which there is no single obvious solution. . . .

Step 2: *Determine the cast and chronology.* Next, re-read the case carefully by immersing yourself into the situation and noting the details of what has happened or is happening. Write out the cast of persons involved in the case including their names, personal characteristics, roles or responsibilities, statements attributed to them, attitudes and feelings they reveal, relations with others in the case, and their circles of influence. Likewise, chart with care the chronology or sequence of events in the case. Decisions almost always are affected by time. . . .

Step 3: *Identify the basic issues.* The third step can be compared with an experience in a zoological laboratory. The speciman is chosen, then dissected, and the various parts are identified and related. Then comes the most difficult part, namely, analyzing what you see. In studying a case this means identifying the basic issue or issues. Basic issues are those factors in the case that have provoked the crisis or that call for a decision to be made.

Step 4: *List the possible alternatives.* Once the issues are decided, one should then list the various alternatives available to the decision-maker(s). . . . On occasions during the discussion of a case someone will say, "We don't have all the information we need to make a decision." In real life we never have all the information we need, and decisions have to be made on the basis of the information available. Only God is omniscient.

. . . .

5: *Participate in the discussion of the case.* To those who readily participate in group discussion, a word of caution is in order. Avoid dominating the discussion. Give the more reserved members an opportunity to speak. To those who are by nature reluctant to disclose their thinking and points of view, a word of encouragement is needed. Speak up. Share your understanding, insights, and conclusions.

. . . .

Case studies done well are a participatory means of learning whereby the effectiveness of the class session depends upon careful preparation by the participants, teacher and students, and during which time everyone in the class enters into the discussion by sharing his or her knowledge and perspective.

Session I: Spirit and Forms of Mission

Goals
1. To develop a working definition of mission.
2. To build community in class by getting acquainted and sharing.
3. To articulate personal images and motivations for mission.

Focus
Mission is more than "program"; it is the nature of the church. The form of mission has changed depending on the time and place in history and the cultural context in which it has taken place.

Text
Preface and chapter 1, "Eve of a New Millennium"

Preparation
Class participants need to feel welcome. This can be accomplished in several ways. Art work (e.g., banners, photographs, names of famous missionaries, globes and/or maps) representing various forms of mission can be displayed on the walls or around the room. Chairs can be arranged to encourage conversation between class members.

Prepare a "graffiti page" by placing a sheet of newsprint on a wall or tripod. In the center of the newsprint write the word "MISSION." Encourage early arrivers to add responses or insights to this graffiti page.

Worshipful Work
For this first session, use a lighted candle to symbolize God's presence throughout the ages. Use actual time pieces or pictures of time pieces that have been used in history (e.g., clocks, sundials, digital clocks, calendars) as illustrations of how we have changed the methods or forms for doing a particular task without changing the essence of the task. Explain that the same is true for mission. The Christian church has always been in mission, but the forms and methods used over twenty centuries have changed considerably.

Read Mark 2:21-22. Sing "God of Love and God of Power" (*United Methodist Hymnal* #578) or "Many Gifts, One Spirit" (*United Methodist Hymnal* #114).

Learning through Involvement

Select the activities that most closely fit your class situation. Determination of activities will be affected by class size, room setting, and your comfort level in leading activities. Remember to use multiple forms of participation and presentation.

Information and Discussion

A. Ask class members to remember and/or review "The Transfiguration of Mission" and "Missional Church." Ask them to define the following: mission, missiology, relevant, sending church, and Christendom. How is your congregation engaged in "relevant" mission?

B. Shenk says that in 1800, 86 percent of all Christians were white Europeans. By 2000, 60 percent will be in Asia, Africa, and Latin America. How might this change our definition or plans for mission?

C. Guder says that most mission committees spend time determining how to divide or allocate the mission budget instead of viewing the entire congregational budget as an exercise in mission. What would happen in your congregation if the mission committee viewed the whole budget as missional?

D. What does Bishop De Carvalho mean by his statement that "these are new times and we shall simply refuse to drink 'old wines in old wineskins'"?

Community Response

If you have asked class members to bring symbols of mission that are indicative of their congregation's ministry or of their personal involvement in mission, let them share these symbols with the group.

Benediction

Share Bishop De Carvalho's perception of how mission has changed in his country. It could be read as it is written, or a litany could be shaped, such as the one below, using his images and the meter of Matthew 25.

> Thanks be to God.
> When you saw people in need of good news, you preached the word.
> When you saw people who could not read, you opened schools, became teachers.
> When you saw sickness and disease, you opened clinics, sent doctors and nurses.
> When you saw oppressive regimes, you joined in liberation and empowerment.

When you saw war, you taught reconciliation.
When you saw land destroyed by mines, you . . .

Sing or read "Lord, You Give the Great Commission" (*United Methodist Hymnal* #584). Let the people say, "Amen."

Assignment for next session
Read chapter 2, "The Sent People of God."

If you plan to use the case study, ask the class to reread it so that they are prepared to discuss it. Have three people volunteer to be Janie and Mitchell Hutchison and Richard Farmer so that they can enact the story or at least describe the situation from their perspectives.

If you plan to have the "Back to the Future" meeting ask for volunteers to be Clementina Butler (see Robert article) and Pauli Murray (see Dharmaraj article) and a UMW president.

Session II: Crossing Barriers for Christ

Goals
1. To understand the changing pattern of sending and receiving missionaries and the necessity of crossing borders and barriers for Christ, remembering that borders and barriers are within our country as well as between nations.
2. To appreciate the unique role women have played in mission.
3. To explore how the gospel becomes rooted in each culture but should never be absorbed by it.

Focus
1. Women bring many gifts to mission.
2. *Contextualization* is a key element in an effective mission strategy.

Text
Chapter 2, "The Sent People of God"

Preparation
Make another graffiti page with the word "MISSIONARY" in the center. Invite those who arrive early to add their thoughts or word associations.

Have four global maps available to construct for the class the "The Christian Church Grows Serially" (see page 25). If you can find maps without color it would be helpful. Otherwise, have available self-adhesive dots or construction paper, scissors, and a glue stick.

If possible, arrange the chairs so that half of the participants have their backs to the other half. If that is not possible, create a barrier through part of the room.

Create a space for class members to place their "unique gifts" from women in mission. The space might be a table or a basket with cardboard women figures on either end. One could be identified as the Samaritan woman and the other as Mother Teresa. The basket or table could be marked "2000 Years of Witnessing." If three-dimensional items do not work in the room, a drawing on a bulletin board would suffice. Have inexpensive "gift bags" ready for class members to name and visibly offer the gifts from women in mission.

Worshipful Work

Try to have new images each time the class gathers. This will help participants to have a new awareness of God's call each day. In addition to a lighted candle, you might have a replica of a small well, musical instruments, or symbols of cultures in other countries.

Read the story of the Samaritan woman at the well (John 4:7-42). Sing the words from "Women" by Mary Sparkes Wheeler, quoted in Dana Robert's article, to the tune "Faithfulness" (*United Methodist Hymnal* #140; hint: it makes three verses without the refrain.) Another option is "Jesus Met the Woman at the Well."

Learning through Involvement

A. Having read the articles by Robert and Dharmaraj, invite class members to name a unique gift that women have contributed to mission. If you have prepared a three-dimensional display, participants may actually go to the table or basket and place their "gift bags" with the names of these gifts written on them. If a bulletin board or wall space is used, have the class members write their words on sticky notes and attach them to the display. The goal is to have these contributions of women, which have often been hidden, to be named and viewed. Once the gifts are named, invite the class to discuss any surprises or new insights they had as they read these particular articles.

B. Create a "Back to the Future" meeting by having persons role play Clementina Butler (an early missionary and organizer of women's missionary societies) and Pauli Murray (a lawyer and mission staff person who compiled information in *States' Laws on Race and Color*), and a UMW president. The "meeting" is to plan and suggest new "borders" that need to be crossed by the women in mission today.

C. Divide the class into four groups. One group will be Christians in 100 C.E., another in 500, another in 1500, and another in 2000. Ask each group to take one of the world maps and color code the center of Christianity for their era. They may use the maps on page 25 of the study book. After each group has shared with the whole group, lead

Jesus Met the Woman at the Well

By Peter Yarrow, Mary Travers & Milton Okun

1.   D   D7
   Jesus met the woman at the well
      G   D
   Jesus met the woman at the well
     G   F#   Bm
   Jesus met the woman at the well
          E   E7   A A7
   And He told her everything she'd ever done.

2. He said, "Woman, where is your husband?"
He said, "Woman, where is your husband?"
He said, "Woman, where is your husband?"
And I know everything you've ever done.

3. She said, "Jesus, I have no husband."
She said, "Jesus, I have no husband."
She said, "Jesus, I have no husband."
And you don't know everything
I've ever done.

4. He said, "Woman, you've had five husbands."
He said, "Woman, you've had five husbands."
He said, "Woman, you've had five husbands."
And the one you have now is not your own.

5. She said, "This man must be a prophet."
She said, "This man must be a prophet."
She said, "This man must be a prophet."
'Cause He told me everything
I've ever done.

Adapted and Arranged by Peter Yarrow, Mary Travers and Milton Okun ©1964 (Renewed) Papemar Music Corp. All rights reserved. Used by permission of Warner Bros. Publications U.S. Inc., Miami, FL 33014.

"We don't have to beg the Lord to be anywhere. The Lord's already there. Just help us be open."

the class in discussing what these maps say about past mission-sending patterns. What are the implications for the next century?

D. Explore the case study "Singing the Lord's Song." If dramatizing the case, use three scenes: (1) Janie and Mitch talking about the importance of indigenous music and the lack of openness of the other missionaries; (2) Mitch and Richard talking about Mitch's concern and Richard's response; (3) mission meeting in which Richard calls on Mitch to defend his work with music and instruments.

Information and Discussion

A. List on a board or newsprint the three pattern changes that Newbigin names in his article "The Pattern of the Christian World Mission": (1) reversal of the tides of world power; (2) renaissance of other world faiths besides Christianity; (3) former "mission" or "younger" churches have matured and will be the center for missionary activity in the next century. What implications will these have for our understanding of mission? About sending and receiving missionaries? (Ask class members to find stories in *New World Outlook* and *Response* that illustrate these points. The stories of particular mission schools, colleges and universities in countries outside the U.S. could be used as illustrations.

B. Of the statistics listed by Dharmaraj, which surprised you the most? How can you as a United Methodist make your concerns known? Where can you join others to act to change these situations?

C. Distribute copies of the Charter on Racial Justice Policies. What additional barriers could be overcome if these were posted in your local church?

D. What does "contextualization" mean? Consult Jacobs's article for clarification. A friend of mine, who grew up in south Texas, remembers having to cut out paper snowflakes at Christmas. Having never seen a snowflake, she thought it must be related to Bethlehem where Jesus was born. As an adult, she found out that that was not true. So why did her teachers want her to cut out snowflakes every Christmas? What does this imply about "contextualizing" the incarnation?

Community Response

Invite participants to comment on the barrier that was created in the room. Has it bothered anyone? Has anyone tried to change it or eliminate it? What are the barriers we have in our lives? Where are they in our communities? Are they in our churches?

Benediction

In recognition of the gifts we receive from others, and if you have used the case study, close by singing one or two African songs from *Global Praise*. Two possibilities are "Amen siakudumisa" (Sing Amen: We praise your name, O God) or "Jesu tawa pano" (Jesus, we are here.) An additional or alternate song is "Jesu, Jesu" (*United Methodist Hymnal* #432). These words are by missionary Tom Colvin who used a melody from a Ghanaian folk song. Verses 2 and 3 have particular relevance for today's lesson.

Distribute to each participant a plain shoestring on which you have printed the initials WWFW (Women's Work for Women) in fabric paint (available at most craft stores.) This is done to remember our sisters in many parts of our world who have no one to speak for them. As participants tie them on their neighbors' wrists, they can hum "Just as I Am" (*United Methodist Hymnal* #357). When all have shoestring bracelets, they can join in saying or singing verse 6:

> *Just as I am, thy love unknown*
> *hath broken every barrier down;*
> *now, to be thine, yea, thine alone,*
> *O Lamb of God, I come, I come.*

Assignment for next session

Read chapter 3, "A Shifting Global Context."

Ask for six volunteers to form a panel to talk about the trends identified by Skreslet. Meet with them after class and have each select one of the topics.

If you plan to use the case study, ask the class to reread it so that it might be fresh in their minds for the discussion.

Session III: The World Is My Parish

Goals

1. To examine the current context for global mission, including views of the North American church and trends that will take us into the next century.
2. To see the North American church as others may view it.
3. To look at how we as Christians, particularly as United Methodists, respond to a "shared stage" with other living faiths and at the impact that has within the United States as well as globally.

Text
Chapter 3, "A Shifting Global Context"

Preparation
1. Have six seats in front for the panelists.
2. On the graffiti page write the following sentence:
   The church of every place
   is a mission-sending church,
   is a mission-receiving church.

   Encourage class members to respond to this global mission statement.
3. Arrange for playing the video spots from United Methodist Communications.

Worshipful Work
For this session place on the table a cross, a globe, a mirror, and, if possible, a hologram. As the world turns, or spins, or wobbles, the cross remains our focal point. The mirror reminds us that, in the past, we have sometimes expected the world to reflect our culture and values. Perhaps the world is now holding a mirror up for us, so that we might see ourselves as others see us.

The hologram reminds us that all of the parts make up the whole, but also that the whole can be seen in every part, no matter how small. Perhaps that is the real truth about Christians and Christianity. The whole body is many members, and yet within every Christian one can witness the wholeness and vastness of God's grace and mercy.

Read Romans 12:9-17. Sing "This Is My Song" (*United Methodist Hymnal* #437). Listen to a recording of "Credo"; the first line begins "I believe in a God, one only" (*Global Praise*).

Learning through Involvement
A. Ask the first person to arrive to be a "person-on-the-street" interviewer, asking other members, "Where do you go to church?" (If all are from the same church, the interviewer may ask, "Did you go to church last Sunday?") He or she should make a notation of any who want to claim that their church is not in *one* place. When all have assembled, ask if this question seemed unusual. Is Hunsberger correct that we define church as "place?" How does that fit with the "sending" motif of mission?

B. View the United Methodist Communications video spots. They show a hurricane setting, an urban homeless ministry, and migrant schools. Each one concludes with the church being "in action" so that "people without a prayer have one."

C. Introduce with a flourish the distinguished panel members who will share their observations on "Emerging Trends in the Global Context." Each one will have two minutes to share his or her observations based on the Skreslet article. Ask the class to respond to the panel. Do you agree with them? What is the basis for affirming or rejecting their perceptions? What else do you want to know? Will these trends affect the way you think about the world and global mission? (For instance, how do we deemphasize the "American" in American mission if the U.S. is seen as the sole superpower? What is the role of the U.S. church in reconciliation if the U.S. is also the primary armed force? Are there subtle shifts in our self-identity if we define ourselves as NGOs rather than the body of Christ?)

D. Introduce the case study, "What's the Matter, Abdaraman?" (pronounced Ab-DAR-a-man). Ask each person to take a partner. One will pantomime the role of Abdaraman, the other Carlo, while the leader summarizes the case study and reads Abdaraman's outburst about his tears and fears. What is Carlo's response? Repeat the process with the partners exchanging roles.

E. As class members share their responses as "Carlo," list them on a writing board or newsprint. Use the SOCs model (Situation, Options, Consequences) for selecting a course of action. The case study is the situation; the options from the group are listed for everyone to see. Go to each suggestion and ask what would be the consequence of that action for Carlo? for Abdaraman? for the Christian witness in Algeria? Is there one answer that seems most helpful?

Information and Discussion

A. Identify your response to Thangaraj's experience in a Hindu temple and Ganga's experience in a United Methodist church. Do you see the rise of other faiths in your community or state? How is your church responding?

B. Walk the class through Thangaraj's explication of John 14:6. What new insights do you find in this reading? How might this be helpful in the case study?

C. Much of today's writing on interfaith concerns states that either we "convert" those who are not Christian or we "dialogue" in a way that excludes any invitation to change, lest it be seen as evidence of the arrogance of Western culture. Is that accurate? If so, what other options do we have?

Community Response
Reread Krister Stendahl's analysis of how we often compare ourselves to others (in the introduction to chapter 3). Do you agree with Stendahl? What things do we compare by describing the "ideal" of our values and the "actuality" of another (e.g., political parties, schools, other faiths, other denominations, size of churches)?

Benediction
Close with "Help Us Accept Each Other" (*United Methodist Hymnal* #560) or "I Believe in a God" (from *Global Praise*).

Assignment for next session
Read chapter 4, "Missional Challenges for the 21st Century."

In order to prevent a "North American only" perspective in class discussion, ask each class member to take on a "dual citizenship." This could be done through a sign-up sheet with the options listed. Using the global map that shows where The United Methodist Church is in mission, ask each class member to identify a country of interest and to write her or his name after that country's name on the sign-up sheet. Or if you would like to do this more randomly, simply put the names of countries into a bowl and ask each member to draw one out. A suggested proportion (based on ten in a class) is as follows: 2 countries from Asia; 3 from Africa; 3 from Latin America and the Caribbean; 2 from Europe. Since everyone will be dual citizens, U.S. concerns will be present as well.

Ask students to use the *Prayer Calendar* and articles from *New World Outlook* and *Response* magazines to find what ministries The United Methodist Church has in their newly adopted "countries." What issues of mission are important to them?

Session IV: The Challenge

Goals
1. To examine the multiple challenges for mission as we enter a new century and a new millennium.
2. To assist class participants in naming and finding a meaningful way each can respond in mission.

Focus
Globalization, distribution of wealth, caring for the broken, the poor, children, the earth, and the changing context for the church in Cuba.

try to climb up, but the rocks and reels makes the go - ing tough just say
prayer is for help, but you stand a - lone feel - ing by your - self, just say

move moun - tain, move moun - tain, moun - tain get out of my way.

(special ending)

If you have faith the size of a mus - tard seed just say

move moun - tain, move moun - tain, move moun - tain, move

(to Coda last time) 1. D.C.   2. D.S. al Coda

moun - tain get out of my way.   way.   just say

CODA

way.

FINE

Words and music by Margaret Pleasant Douroux,
Rev. Earl A. Pleasant Publishing © 1983. All rights reserved.
Used by permission.

Text

Chapter 4, "Missional Challenges for the 21st Century"

Preparation

1. On a graffiti page write the phrase "2001: A World of Mission." Encourage early arrivers to jot down thoughts about mission in our world.
2. Prepare sheets for the cinquain poetry.
3. Make banners from the quotations used in "Worshipful Work."

Worshipful Work

In front of a cross, place symbols of distractions, such as a blank checkbook, a cell phone and/or hand-held computer, a toy soldier, and a photo of a mountain. There are times when we place more energy into obtaining these nonessentials than in viewing the cross or in being faithful to our God.

Americans have a saying, "Behind every cloud is a silver lining." In Haiti there is a saying, "Behind every mountain is another mountain." Does it ever feel that way for us?

Read (or have various class members read) selected verses, such as Mark 11:23 (moving mountains), Matthew 6:19 (treasures on earth), Matthew 18:3 (become like children). Sing "Jesus Loves the Little Children" and "Santo, Santo, Santo" (from *Global Praise*) or "Move, Mountain."

Learning through Involvement

A. Create a simulation in which the class becomes a conference session (general or annual conference) or a church council in which they are asked to adopt the mission agenda for the next quadrennium (four years) or for the next decade.

The following activities can be done independently from this simulation or as the first steps in the simulation.

B. Divide the class into four to six smaller groups. Let each group choose one issue from chapter 4 that they want to make sure gets on the "Mission Agenda 2000." (This will work best if no two groups have the same issue.) Give them time to examine resource materials if needed. Ask them to present their issue to the class by writing cinquain poetry. Cinquain poetry has five lines and is usually written with these guidelines:

line one: one word, the subject (usually a noun)
line two: two words, describing the subject (usually adjectives)
line three: three words, action words about the subject (usually verbs)

line four: a four-word phrase, describing one's feelings about the subject
line five: one word, response to the subject

An example (from *Great Mission Ideas for Workers with Children* by Faye Wilson):

Refugees
Homeless millions
hungering, waiting, hoping
wanting to be neighbors
Liberty

C. Remembering their "dual" citizenship, give class members time to confer with others from the same continent. They may share their cinquains with one another. With a different context in mind, would a different issue take priority? Would they like to work for two issues?

D. As the leader, you may determine if this simulation produces a petition for general conference, and therefore for the whole denomination, or a resolution for the annual conference, therefore needing funding by the churches of the conference. It may be a local church committee who wants to make sure the millennium celebration has a missional focus. Use the setting that will generate the most energy for your setting. Choose someone to preside. Let the class have an honest time to set what they believe to be the most urgent "Mission Agenda 2000."

E. Use the case study. Have the class become the long-range planning committee for the Cuban congregation. What has contributed to its remarkable growth and vitality? Identify the factors that most influence your decision on the future role of the church in Cuba.

Look at the maps in chapter 4 that contrast income and population. How do these factors affect the churches in the Caribbean? Although the political context is different, do any class members have the experience of being in a church that has said it wanted to grow, but acted more as if it did not want to change? Do any communities of faith in the U.S. struggle between being a *church* that ministers to the needy and being a *social agency* in the public's perception? What insights can be shared? (If time is short in this session, this case study and simulation can be accomplished in session 5.)

Information and Discussion

A. Reread "Church in a Market Economy." Does it sound like any church you know? If so, what can we do to change it? Does the contrast of the map of income/affluence and the map of population give a unique agenda for the churches in the U.S. and Europe?

B. Mercy Oduyoye graphically calls to mind the image of various African cultures that is portrayed through the U.S. public media. She says, "The mission of the future church is to respond to all the poverties of humanity, and there is none so poor as the one who does not feel any need." How can we acknowledge our own poverty and stand in solidarity with children and women who are marginalized in their own cultures? What steps can we take to prevent the manipulation of images through the public media?

C. Harold Recinos asks us to see racism as a worldview. Additionally, he wants us to see the colorful diversity in our country. Much of our reconciling work on racism has centered around black-white issues. In turning to multiethnic diversity and the rise in the number of Hispanics and Asians in the U.S., we must also look at language ministries. Are we prepared both to accept the diversity and to find new ways to be more than a one-language church? John Wesley's "the world is my parish," has become for United Methodism "the world in our parish."

D. Messer assures us that there are no nonpersons in God's family. He uses as examples persons that our society chooses to overlook, namely persons with HIV/AIDS or persons with Alzheimer's. Are there others? When do you find yourself looking straight ahead so that you won't encounter someone? Does that make that individual a "nonperson?" How does this article correlate to Anthony's view of heaven and Isabel's feeling of being "put in a garage" in Kozol's interview with the children of Harlem and the Bronx?

Community Response

Sing "Tú Has Venido a la Orilla" (Lord, You Have Come to the Lakeshore; *United Methodist Hymnal* #344). If participants feel they cannot sing the entire song in Spanish, then focus on singing the chorus in Spanish. Reflect on how it feels not to be able to understand what is being said or how embarrassed we feel when we mispronounce words.

Benediction

Recall Mary Previte's affirmation that God gives us the ability to change mountains. Have class members read the following quotes:

I am not here to please the dominant culture. I live to please my Lord and Savior. My spiritual tastebuds have graduated from fizz and froth to Fire and Ice. Don't give me that old-time religion. Don't give me that new-time religion. Give me that all-time religion that is as hard as rock and soft as snow. . . .

I won't back down, slow down, shut down, or let down until I'm preached out, teached out, healed out, hauled out of God's mission in the world entrusted to members of the Church of the Out-of-Control . . . to unbind the confined, whether they're the downtrodden or the upscale, the overlooked or the under-represented.
—From Leonard Sweet, "A Cup of Coffee at the Soul Cafe"[3]

O Lord, some of us have mites
    and some of us have millions
        and most of us fall somewhere in between.
We know it's our responsibility to give from what we've been given,
    and Jesus made it very clear that
        it was not the size of the gift,
            but the size of the giver's heart that matters.
You, O Lord, know our treasures and our hearts.
May our hearts swell to the occasion!"
—From Ann Weems, *Searching for Shalom*[4]

Assignment for next session
1. Collect the cinquains to use in the next session.
2. Read Chapter 5, "Our Engagement in Mission."
3. Research ways that the Mission Agenda 2000 can be implemented effectively. What ministries, projects, agencies, or organizations can be coalesced to make a dynamic difference in the next decade? Ask each person to come back with at least two ideas for the implementation of the Agenda.

Session V: The Car Is Not Empty

Goals
1. To feel personally called to be a part of God's mission.
2. To sense our investment in the global nature and inclusive community of The United Methodist Church.

Focus

The sharing of one's faith, not as "top down" or "rich to poor," but as a natural response to the love of Christ.

Text

Chapter 5, "Our Engagement in Mission"

Preparation

1. On a graffiti page write the statement: "These are new times and we shall simply refuse to drink old wine in old wineskins."
2. Post the cinquains around the room. Have materials from the General Board of Global Ministries that speak of the multiple ways persons can be in mission.
3. Prepare acrostic sheets.

Worshipful Work

1. Use the following visual symbols: a cross, a lighted candle, bread, and colorful pieces of paper each with the name of one of the class members written on it.
2. Ask two class members to enact the phone conversations between Tex and his mother-in-law (see p.98). We are called by name, but even the best of us need to be trained to be in mission.
3. Read John 21:15-17, then the following reflection:

> He said, "Feed my sheep."
>> There were no conditions:
>>> Least of all, Feed my sheep if they deserve it.
>>> Feed my sheep if you feel like it.
>>> Feed my sheep if you have any leftovers.
>>> Feed my sheep if the mood strikes you,
>>>> if the economy's OK . . .
>>>> if you're not too busy . . .
>> No conditions . . . just, "Feed my sheep."
> Could it be that God's Kingdom will come
>> when each lamb is fed?
> We who have agreed to keep covenant
>> are called to feed sheep
>>> even when it means the grazing will be done
>>>> on our own front lawns.
>
> —From Ann Weems, *Searching for Shalom* [5]

We are all at the foot of the cross, called by name to let our light shine and to "feed" his sheep. Sing "We Are the Church," verses 1,2, and 4 (*United Methodist Hymnal* #558).

Learning through Involvement

A. Look at the Mission Agenda 2000. Have persons report on how these ministries can be actively implemented, not just in theory but in each community and through every congregation. Some may be timeless, such as prayer, love offerings, acts of charity. Some may be for this moment in history, such as combating hate crimes, responding to AIDS crises, evangelism in urban and multilingual arenas.

B. Case studies: If the Cuba case study was not used previously, it could be used in this session as the class looks again at the issue of globalization and our connectional Wesleyan ministries. Have the class simulate a meeting of the long-range planning committee to see which options might be the most helpful and realistic for this witnessing community.

Or use the case study, "A Church for All People?" in chapter 5. How much diversity is possible within a single congregation? Even if class members have never had the experience of being in an international congregation, they may understand well the kinds of diversity that exist in a rural, small-town, or suburban church, or in a congregation in a transitional neighborhood, or in a congregation with a changing age range or economic status.

C. Discuss what the Escobar and Harman reflections imply about the relationship of the U.S. churches to the Methodist Church in Cuba and other Latin American churches.

D. Poitras speaks of the joy in mission. Have the class (in teams of two or three) complete an acrostic. To do this, use the letters below, to form the first word of their poem or other composition.

J
O
Y

I
N

M
I
S
S
I
O
N

For example:

Jesus taught us to care about
Others.
Your actions will reflect God's love....

Information and Discussion

A. Use Newbigin's five points on mission evangelism as a true/false test. Read a statement and have the class call out "true" or "false." Where are there dissenting opinions? Are we as United Methodists engaged effectively in evangelism?

B. Is The United Methodist Church still active in mission? Looking back at the Delaney and Jacob articles in chapter 2, as well as the articles in chapter 5, what is the impact of the development of strong indigenous leadership and the Volunteers in Mission program on the ongoing mission personnel program? Can anyone name the new mission personnel programs that have been announced through the General Board of Global Ministries?

C. What does it mean to be a community witness as distinct from an individual witness? What will it mean for our mission strategy if we live in a country where, as Christians, we are a minority, rather than the cultural majority?

Community Response

Place the cinquains around the room. Give class members time to circulate, read them, and sign their names on any sheet that names a missional issue they are personally willing to address.

Benediction

Have members share their acrostics.

Stand in a circle in close proximity to one another and to the Worshipful Work space. One person begins by going to the Worshipful Work space, picking up one of the pieces of paper with a name on it (not one's own) and lifting up that servant's name for God's blessing, perhaps by saying "God bless _____ as she/he goes forth as your servant in mission." Continue around the circle until each person goes by the cross and picks out a person's name. The class may hum "Here I Am, Lord" (*United Methodist Hymnal* #593).

In unison, pray the prayer of Ignatius of Loyola (*United Methodist Hymnal* #570):

> Teach us, good Lord,
> to serve you as you deserve;
> to give and not to count the cost;
> to fight and not to heed the wounds;
> to toil and not to seek for rest;
> to labor and not to ask for any reward,
> except that of knowing that we do your will;
> through Jesus Christ our Lord.
>   Amen.

2. The Sent People of God

1. Tracey K. Jones Jr., *Our Mission Today: The Beginning of a New Age* (New York: World Outlook Press, 1963), 107.

2. D. March (1816-1909), "Hark! The Voice of Jesus Crying" in Charles Clayton Morrison and Herbert L. Willett, eds. *Hymns of the United Church* (Christian Century Press, 1925).

3. Mrs. L. H. Daggett, *Historical Sketches of Woman's Missionary Societies in America and England* (Boston: Mrs. L. H. Daggett, 1879), 43.

4. Ibid., 48.

5. Patricia R. Hill, *The World Their Household: The American Woman's Foreign Missionary Movement and Cultural Transformation, 1870-1920* (Ann Arbor: University of Michigan Press, 1985), 3.

6. Quoted in Dorothy Robins-Mowry, "Not a Foreigner, but a Sensei—a Teacher: Nannie B. Gaines of Hiroshima," in Leslie Flemming, ed., *Women's Work for Women: Missionaries and Social Change in Asia* (Boulder, Colo.: Westview Press, 1989), 106.

7. Dorothy Clarke Wilson, *Dr. Ida: Passing on the Torch of Life* (New York: Friendship Press, 1976), 29-46.

8. Saleni Armstrong-Hopkins, *Within the Purdah* (New York: Eaton & Mains, 1898), 8.

9. Interview with Julia Reed Paxton.

10. *Report of the Ecumenical Conference on Foreign Missions*, vol. 1 (New York: American Tract Society, 1900), 215.

11. Thelma Stevens, *Legacy for the Future: The History of Christian Social Relations in the Women's Division of Christian Service, 1940-1968* (New York: Women's Division, Board of Global Ministries, United Methodist Church, 1978), 37.

12. Ibid., 61.

13. United Nations Development Programme, *Human Development Report* (New York: Oxford University Press, 1995), 1010.

14. United Nations Development Programme, *Human Development Report* (New York: Oxford University Press, 1996), 21-24.

15. United Nations Development Programme, *Human Development Report* (New York: Oxford University Press, 1997), 3-5, 29-32.

16. Quoted in Daniel Von Allmen, "The Birth of Theology: Contextualization as the Dynamic Element in the Formation of New Testament Theology," *International Review of Mission* 64 (253): 37-52.

17. Ibid., 39.

18. Willem A. Visser 't Hooft, "Accommodation—True or False," *South East Asia Journal of Theology* (1967): 6.

3. A Shifting Global Context

1. Kanzo Uchimura, "Can Americans Teach Japanese in Religion?" *Japan Christian Intelligencer* 1 (1926): 357-61.

2. Ibid., 357.

3. "The Time for the World's Conversion Come" first appeared in the *Religious Magazine*, Boston, in 1837-38. This quotation is from pages 65-66 of the article as it was reprinted in *To Advance the Gospel: Selections from the Writings of Rufus Anderson*, ed. R. Pierce Beaver (Grand Rapids: Eerdmans, 1967), 59-70.

4. These six lectures were given in April 1991 at Western Theological Seminary in Holland, Michigan. There are audio and videotapes of the lectures in the seminary's library.

5. Samuel P. Huntington, "The Clash of Civilizations," *Foreign Affairs* 72 (Summer 1993): 22.

6. Robert D. Kaplan, "The Coming Anarchy," *Atlantic Monthly* 273 (February 1994): 70.

7. These remarks were reported without direct attribution by Saadeddin Ibrahim, director of the Cairo, Egypt-based Ibn Khaldun Centre for Development Studies, in *Al-Ahram Weekly* 211 (9-15 March 1995): 9.

8. An adapted version of Fogel's lecture was published in the *Wall Street Journal*, 9 January 1996, A14.

4. Missional Challenges for the 21st Century

1. Charles W. Kegley Jr. and Eugene R. Wittkopf., *World Politics: Trend and Transformation* (New York: St. Martin's Press, 1997), 249.

2. Benjamin R. Barber, *Jihad vs. McWorld: How Globalization and Tribalism Are Reshaping the World* (New York: Ballantine, 1995), 5.

3. Roger Finke and Rodney Stark, *The Churching of America, 1776-1990: Winners and Losers in Our Religious Economy* (New Brunswick, N.J.: Rutgers University Press, 1992), 17.

4. Excerpted from "Mission Reflection and Mission Action", the address of the general secretary to the annual meeting of the General Board of Global Ministries, October 20, 1997.

5. Audrey Smedley, *Race in North America: Origin and Evolution of a Worldview* (Boulder, Colo.: Westview Press, 1993), 36-40.

6. Ibid., 21.

7. Lee Romney and Jeff Brazil, "Boy's Death Stirs Debate over California's Immigration Initiative," *Washington Post*, 25 November 1994, A3.

8. *UN Chronicle* 32 (June 1995): 59.

9. Frederick C. Cuny, "Refugees, Displaced Persons, and the United Nations System," in *U.S. Foreign Policy and the United Nations System*, ed. Charles W. Maynes and Richard S. Williamson (New York: Norton, 1996), 188.

10. Leonard Sweet, *Quantum Spirituality: A Postmodern Apologetic* (Dayton, Ohio: Whaleprints, 1991), 300.

11. Cited in Lawrence E. Joseph, *Gaia: The Growth of an Idea* (New York: St. Martin's Press, 1990), 1.

12. James Lovelock, *The Ages of Gaia: A Biography of Our Living Earth* (New York: Bantam Books, 1990), 27.

13. The names and occupations are taken from "One Year in the Epidemic: The Faces of AIDS," *Newsweek*, 10 August 1987, 24-31.

14. Norman Cousins, *AGB Reports*, March/April 1980, 38.

15. Cited in "New WCC Mission Director Notes Priorities Ahead," *Ecumenical Press Service*, 16 June 1989, 1.

16. *The State of the World's Children* (UNICEF, 1995).

17. Henry D. Rack, *Reasonable Enthusiast: John Wesley and the Rise of Methodism* (Nashville: Abingdon Press, 1992), 533.

18. Richard P. Heitzenrater, *Wesley and the People Called Methodists* (Nashville: Abingdon Press, 1995), 105-6.

19. Ibid., 232.

20. See Wesley's essay, "Thoughts upon Methodism," dated August 4, 1787, and his sermon, "On God's Vineyard," written in 1787 after Wesley visited the societies across England.

5. Our Engagement in Mission

1. William R. Read, *New Patterns of Church Growth in Brazil* (Grand Rapids: Eerdmans, 1965), 121.

2. Paul Freston, "Uma Breve Historia do Pentecostalismo Brasileiro. Parte 1: A Assembleia de Deus." Unpublished paper presented at the Second Inter-American Missiological Consultation, Buenos Aires, Argentina, 1992, p. 2.

3. Orlando E. Costas, *Liberating News* (Grand Rapids: Eerdmans, 1989), 49.

4. Ibid., 67.

5. Nikolai Berdyaev, *The Origins of Russian Communism* (London: Centenary Press, 1937), 225-26.

6. Gustavo Gutiérrez, "Joy in the Midst of Suffering," in *Christ and Context: The Confrontation between Gospel and Culture*, ed. Hilary D. Regan and Alan J. Torrance (Edinburgh, Scotland: T & T Clark, 1993), 79.

7. See his *The Responsible Self: An Essay in Christian Moral Philosophy* (New York: Harper and Row, 1963), especially pp. 60-68.

Study Guide

1. Dick Murray, *Teaching the Bible to Adults and Youth,* rev. and updated (Nashville: Abingdon Press, 1993), 31.

2. Harvey Cox quote in the introduction to the study guide. From *Seductionof the Spirit*, 1973, p.277, quoted in *The Globalization of Communications: Some Religious Implications* by Chris Arthur (WCC Publications, Geneva, 1998), 48.

3. Leonard Sweet, "A Cup of Coffee at the Soul Café," as quoted in a sermon by Reverend Aaron Brown, pastor, St. Paul UMC, Joplin, Missouri, August 30, 1998.

4. Ann Weems, "Where Your Treasure Is . . .," in *Searching for Shalom: Resources for Creative Worship* (Louisville, KY: Westminster/John Knox Press, 1991), 72.

5. Ann Weems, "Feeding Sheep," in *Searching for Shalom: Resources for Creative Worship* (Louisville, KY: Westminster/John Knox Press, 1991), 47.

Dr. Rena M. Yocom currently serves as Director of Gospel Communication for the Louisiana Area of The United Methodist Church. She is vice-president of the World Association for Christian Communication and president of the North America Regional Association. She has served as chair of the Board of Publications for the American Society of Missiology. She co-edited *Church in the Movement of the Spirit* and was a contributing author to *Women and Church, Twelve Tales Untold,* and *Sabbath.*

Dr. Yocom is a deacon in full connection in the Louisiana Conference. Her graduate degrees are from Saint Paul School of Theology and San Francisco Theological Seminary. During her seven years as an associate general secretary at the General Board of Global Ministries, she coordinated two Global Gatherings. She has served in local churches, taught in conference and regional schools of Christian mission, conducted a course of study for local pastors, and led workshops around the globe.

Order all resources by stock number from the Service Center.
Please mail order with check payable to:
SERVICE CENTER
P.O. BOX 691328
CINCINNATI, OH 45269-1328

COSTS FOR SHIPPING AND HANDLING:

Sale Items:	Free Items:
$25 or less, add $3.50	50 or less, add $2.50
$25.01-$60, add $4.50	51-400, add $3.50
$60.01-$100, add $5.50	Over 400, add 75¢ per 100
Over $100, add 5%	

For billed or credit card orders
CALL TOLL FREE: 1-800-305-9857 FAX ORDERS: 1-513-761-3722
If billing is requested, $1.50 billing fee is charged.
Mail to: SERVICE CENTER, GENERAL BOARD OF GLOBAL MINISTRIES,
THE UNITED METHODIST CHURCH, 7820 READING RD. CALLER NO. 1800
CINCINNATI, OH 45222-1800